GOD
the Holy Trinity

SAMFORD UNIVERSITY

Beeson Divinity Studies
Timothy George, Editor

Beeson Divinity Studies is a series of volumes dedicated to the pastoral and theological renewal of the Church of Jesus Christ. The series is sponsored by the faculty of Beeson Divinity School of Samford University, an evangelical, interdenominational theological school in Birmingham, Alabama.

GOD
the Holy Trinity

Reflections on
Christian Faith and Practice

TIMOTHY GEORGE
EDITOR

Baker Academic
Grand Rapids, Michigan

© 2006 by Timothy George

Published by Baker Academic
a division of Baker Publishing Group
P.O. Box 6287, Grand Rapids, MI 49516-6287
www.bakeracademic.com

Second printing, January 2007

Printed in the United States of America

Library of Congress Cataloging-in-Publication Data
God the Holy Trinity : reflections on Christian faith and practice / Timothy
    George, editor.
        p.   cm.
    Includes bibliographical references and index.
    ISBN 10: 0-8010-2765-9 (pbk.)
    ISBN 978-0-8010-2765-9 (pbk.)
    1. Trinity. I. George, Timothy.
BT111.3.G63 2006
231′.044—dc22   2006018859

For
James M. Houston

O Trinity, O Trinity,
  the uncreated One;
O Unity, O Unity
  of Father, Spirit, Son:
You are without beginning,
Your life is never ending;
    and though our tongues are
      earthbound clay,
    light them with flaming fire today.

From the Lenten Triodion of the Orthodox Church

Contents

Introduction

TIMOTHY GEORGE

When I was a student at Harvard Divinity School during the 1970s, one of my teachers published a book entitled *God the Problem*. This prompted a retort from one of his colleagues: "Those theologians, they can make a problem out of anything!" While reveling in obscurity and complexity may be the delight of some theologians, if there has ever been a genuine "problem" in Christian doctrine, then surely it is how the eternal God can be both One and yet ever Three at the same time. But this is what all orthodox Christians do confess: that the one and only Almighty God who created heaven and earth has forever known himself, and through salvation history has revealed himself to us, as the Father, the Son, and the Holy Spirit. So basic is this belief in the Holy Trinity that it has become one of the essential markers of the Christian faith.

The essays in this volume are part of the rich harvest of trinitarian thinking that has characterized Christian theology for more than seventy-five years now. We must set this revival of trinitarian theology against the backdrop of several centuries that saw declining interest in the doctrine. The Reformation, in both its Protestant and Catholic modalities, remained formally committed to the orthodox trinitarian consensus of the early church. The doctrine of the Trinity was not a matter of dispute between Wittenberg or Geneva and Rome. Most of the radical reformers also affirmed the doctrine of the Trinity, with the exception of a small number of evangelical rationalists such as Michael Servetus, Faustus Socinus, and the Polish Brethren. The two burning issues of the Reformation were soteriology, "What can I do to be saved?" and ecclesiology, "Where can I find a true church?" In his famous maxim "To know Christ is to know his benefits," Philipp Melanchthon well expressed what we might call the soteriological concentration of Reformation theology. Melanchthon and nearly everyone else on both sides of the confessional divide in the sixteenth century assumed a trinitarian framework for their elaborate discussions of justification, predestination, eucharistic theology, and the like. Yet this would not be the case several centuries later, when scholars applied Enlightenment epistemology to the content of Christian theology. Immanuel Kant, for example, claimed that the human mind could know God only as an ordering concept, like the "soul" or the "world." This meant that Christian doctrines such as the Trinity were at best constructs of human consciousness, a mental grid of sorts, certainly not a reality that one could know, appropriate, or enter into in the way the Christian tradition had always claimed. Given these two developments—the soteriological concentration of the Reformation and the Kantian limit upon knowledge claims—it was "merely a matter of logic before trinitarian doctrine found itself on the margins of Christian theology."[1]

The father of modern theology was Friedrich Schleiermacher, who famously defined the Christian religion as "a feeling of absolute dependence." Despite his roots in the Reformed tradition and his strong ties to Moravian Pietism, Schleiermacher was the first great post-Kantian theologian, and his treatment of the doctrine of the Trinity reflects this commitment. In a few paragraphs the Trinity makes a brief appearance at the end of his long doctrinal treatise *The Christian Faith*. The Trinity is not the apex of his thinking but rather an appendix, almost an afterthought. By radically reinterpreting traditional doctrines in the light of Christian self-consciousness, Schleiermacher was able to relativize not only the doctrine of the Trinity but also much of the substance of historic creedal Christianity. Others would go even further. As Jaroslav Pelikan put it, "Schleiermacher's dictum that certain doctrines may be 'entrusted to history for safekeeping' became an axiom by means of which other theologians could assign much of the orthodox tradition to irrelevance."[2]

Karl Barth stands at the headwaters of a renewed interest in the doctrine of the Trinity in the twentieth century. Unlike Schleiermacher, Barth places the doctrine of the Trinity at the beginning of his theological project, in the opening chapters of his *Church Dogmatics*. With Barth, theology begins not with human self-consciousness but rather with God's self-revelation. Human beings on their own are not capable of peering into the mystery of God, but the God of the Bible has spoken—*Deus dixit!*—and this is the basis for our understanding of the Triune God as Revealer, Revelation, and Revealedness (*CD* I/1:295). Because God has made himself known in this way, we can truly know him, Barth says, "in unimpaired unity yet also in unimpaired distinction."[3] Barth's trinitarian thinking has proved enormously fertile for other theologians who, while critical of Barth at key points, have extended his own Christocentric emphasis. Among the most creative and notable theologians in this trajectory are Eberhard Jüngel and Robert Jenson. At the same time, we must recognize that the doctrine of the Trinity remained marginalized in a great swath of Protestant theology. For example, Rudolf Bultmann, one of the most influential theologians of the twentieth century, showed no interest in the Trinity and remained much in the tradition of Schleiermacher on this subject.

Because Roman Catholic theology has retained the substance of creedal Christianity through the centuries, this tradition never seriously questioned the doctrine of the Trinity. This is not to say, however, that there has been no significant development in Roman Catholic trinitarian theology in recent times. In traditional Roman Catholic dogmatics, the doctrine of the Trinity (*De Deo Trino*) was always distinguished and treated separately from the study of God's reality and unity (*De Deo Uno*). As a major corrective to this approach, Karl Rahner declared: "The 'economic' Trinity is the 'immanent' Trinity, and the 'immanent' Trinity is the 'economic' Trinity."[4] It is misleading, Rahner argued, to divorce the reality and unity of the one eternal God from the way this God has manifested himself in the history of salvation. "Father," "Son," and "Holy Spirit" are not mere masks God wears at different moments in history, like the same actor who plays different parts at different times in a three-act play.

Instead, these divine names are a divinely given and accurate depiction of who God actually is. Alister McGrath summarizes this view: "The same God who *appears* as a Trinity *is* a Trinity. The way in which God is known in self-revelation corresponds to the way God is internally."[5]

The early church worked out much of its trinitarian reflection in the East, and the Orthodox tradition has served as the guardian of this dogmatic consensus through the centuries. The major development in Orthodox trinitarian thinking came during the medieval era with the work of Gregory Palamas, who distinguished between the essence and energies of God. However, because the Eastern Church was spared the crises of the Reformation and the Enlightenment, the Trinity remained at the center of our Christian life, being reflected in the rich traditions of iconography, liturgy, and meditation. In recent decades, however, some of the most important contributors to the current trinitarian renaissance have come from the Eastern Church. Among the most notable of these perhaps is John Zizioulas, whose book *Being as Communion* (1985) has made an enormous impact. Zizioulas and other Eastern theologians have once again brought to the fore the teaching of the Cappadocian fathers concerning the *perichōrēsis*, the coinherence of the three divine persons in the Godhead. This motif was never completely lost in the West but tended to remain obscured by those who followed Augustine, and then Aquinas, in moving from a primary emphasis on God's unity to the subsequent discussion of God's tri-unity. The notion that, as Jonathan Edwards once put it, "God is within himself a holy society," has spawned a new interest in the "social Trinity," though some construals of social trinitarianism have moved far beyond the bounds of historic Christian orthodoxy.

The papers published in this volume were originally presented at Beeson Divinity School of Samford University in the symposium "God the Holy Trinity: A Conference on Faith and Christian Life." The speakers represented Roman Catholic, Eastern Orthodox, and Protestant (Anglican, Baptist, Presbyterian, and Holiness) theological traditions. While there are diverse voices and varying emphases in these essays, they represent an underlying commitment to the trinitarian faith of the apostolic tradition, grounded in Holy Scripture and confessed by the early church. None of the contributors to this volume would for a moment minimize the serious theological and ecclesial differences that still, sadly, prevent us as believing Christians from coming together to the banquet of the Lord's Table. But we do recognize one another as brothers and sisters in Jesus Christ, and we stand together in our commitment to the historic trinitarian faith of the church. As an expression of the unity we already have in Christ, for the fullness of which we still wait, we stood together with the congregation assembled for worship in the conference at which these papers were given, and in unison we recited the Nicene Creed.

Another theme runs through all of these essays. While not avoiding some of the sharp issues and debates, we were concerned that we not present the doctrine of the Trinity as a heady theological conundrum, a "problem" to be solved. We wanted to address a crucial question: How does the doctrine of the Trinity shape the ways of the Christian life, its worship and prayer, its service and mission? There is a pastoral theme in this book that highlights the trinitarian shape of spiritual formation.

In the opening chapter, Alister McGrath presents an evangelical reflection of the doctrine of the Trinity. He begins with a call to humility, reminding us that our best theological work on this theme will always fall immeasurably short of the reality with which it is concerned. "Mystery" is an oft-used but appropriate word to describe the God who is both hidden and revealed, the God whom we can never "capture" in any formulation. While McGrath applauds the resurgence of interest in the Trinity, following its long demise in Protestant liberalism, he also sounds a note of caution that the theological pendulum may have swung too far in a trinitarian direction. He leads us to Thomas à Kempis, who disparaged speculation about the Trinity in favor of a love for the Trinity, an affective response that requires conversion and a changed life.

One of the common objections to trinitarian theology, especially within the evangelical tradition, is the belief that it lacks sufficient scriptural warrant. The word *trinitas* is not found in the Bible but was coined by Tertullian many years after the final books of the Bible were written. In his essay, "Out of the Box: The Christian Experience of God in Trinity," Gerald Bray challenges this idea by looking closely at the biblical basis for Christian trinitarian thought. In his exposition of the key verse,

Galatians 4:6, Bray shows how the early church's awareness
of the Trinity stemmed from the basic experience of Christian
worship and prayer: "To confess God as a Trinity is to worship
him in our hearts, as those hearts are stirred by the Spirit of the
Son crying 'Abba, Father.'"

James Earl Massey's essay, "Faith and Christian Life in the
African-American Spirituals," shows how poignant songs from
the time of slavery reflect a deep and palpable response to the
work of God as the Father, the Son, and the Spirit. The role of
the Holy Spirit, often neglected in more scholastic presentations
on the Trinity, comes to the fore in the moans, chants, and yearn-
ings of the spirituals.

Avery Cardinal Dulles looks at the way the doctrine of the Trinity serves as a fundamental bedrock for ecumenical witness and
work. From New Testament times onward, baptism in the name
of the Father, the Son, and the Holy Spirit has been a basic rite of
initiation for the Christian community. As Cyprian put it in the
third century, the church is "a people made one with the unity
of the Father, the Son, and the Holy Spirit." Of special interest
is Dulles's review and critique of Vladimir Soloviev's creative
proposal, seeking a way forward for Christian unity based upon
trinitarian ecclesiology.

Frederica Mathewes-Green is a member of the Antiochian
Orthodox Church, and her presentation reflects the wider concerns of Eastern Christianity. She reminds us that the Trinity is
central in Christian worship and that we often best approach
this subject through the media of art, architecture, and iconography. Her meditation on a famous painting by the Russian
monk Andrei Rublev, entitled "The Old Testament Trinity," draws
together important lessons about the nature and character of
God through this visual interpretation of Genesis 18:1–20. She
concludes her meditation with an exhortation to silence before
the mystery of the holy.

J. I. Packer shows us how trinitarian thinking permeates the
theological work of the great English Puritan John Owen. Packer
rescues Owen from the dour stereotype often applied to all Puritans and presents him instead as a theologian of the heart,
equally concerned with doctrinal and devotional issues. Packer
describes Owen's great book of sermons on communion with God
as a "radically trinitarian account of the inside story of Christian

existence." The Westminster Shorter Catechism declares that the chief end of human existence is "to glorify God and enjoy Him forever." John Owen turns out to be an important spiritual guide in the fulfillment of this goal.

The Trinity has always been a contentious doctrine, not only within Christianity but also in Christianity's engagement with other world religions, especially with the two other great monotheistic traditions, Judaism and Islam. In "The Trinity and the Challenge of Islam," Timothy George examines the Christian-Muslim exchange over the Trinity. Among the issues he tackles is the question of whether Islam, in its formative phase, understood what Christians meant when they declared that God is both One and Three, or whether the quite negative reaction of Islam to the Trinity was really a response to a corrupted version of the doctrine. By confronting the provocative questions "Is monotheism enough?" and "Does God need a Son?" he explores the implications of the Christian understanding of God for Christian-Muslim dialogue today.

In her retrieval of Augustine's doctrine of the Trinity, Ellen T. Charry offers a stout critique of the trajectory of trinitarian theology represented by Barth, and more recently, Robert Jenson and Catherine LaCugna. When they focus so strongly on a communitarian model of the Trinity, sometimes in a socially reductionist way, these thinkers obscure something important about God's divine character. Charry looks at various traits associated with the divine character and concludes that while God's character is not unstable, our ability to understand it is partial. Knowing God well is an art, she says, and a difficult one at that. Alister McGrath opens this volume by sounding the note of mystery; Ellen Charry brings it to a close by reminding us of divine simplicity—an Augustinian perspective that stresses the transformation of the soul by the goodness, wisdom, and beauty of God.

The final chapter of this volume is a sermon by Cornelius Plantinga Jr. on "Deep Wisdom." The Gospel of John has always deeply informed the richest strands of trinitarian theology, and here Plantinga works from several key texts. In the story of Jesus as John tells it, the glory of the one Triune God is manifested in the tangible elements of wine, water, bread, and blood. This is the deep wisdom that finds the power of God and the glory of

God displayed for all the world to see one Friday in Jerusalem, on a hill called Calvary.

Finally, this volume is dedicated, with gratitude and esteem, to James M. Houston, the founding principal of Regent College in Vancouver, and a frequent visiting professor at Beeson Divinity School. Drawing on the wisdom of the Christian tradition in its fullness, he has served the evangelical church by forging a model of spiritual theology and theological education that brings us into the heart of the Holy Trinity so clearly revealed in the face of Jesus Christ.

1

The Doctrine of the Trinity

An Evangelical Reflection

ALISTER E. MCGRATH

One of my fonder childhood memories concerns a church service in Northern Ireland, in the late 1950s. I was growing up, totally disinterested in the Christian faith, but still feeling the cultural pressure to self-identify religiously and attend church. The Book of Common Prayer was still the only authorized form of worship, and we religiously—I think I can safely use that word!—followed its seventeenth-century English prose. On one occasion, for reasons that I cannot entirely recall, we said the Athanasian Creed. As we recited its rather ponderous statements, we came to affirming our belief in "the Father incomprehensible, the Son incomprehensible, and the Holy Ghost incomprehensible." I can still recall the loud voice of a slightly deaf local farmer, standing by my side, booming out: "The whole damn thing's incomprehensible." The congregation had paused for breath at that particular point and had no difficulty in hearing this piece of theological commentary.

At that stage, I have to admit that I had no particular interest in religion, regarding attending church as one of life's less exciting inevitabilities. But some such thought has haunted the Western church throughout its history, particularly since the rise of the "Age of Reason" in the eighteenth century. Is the doctrine of the Trinity simply an intellectual incoherence? Perhaps it is the classic example of an outdated and outmoded demand that we, like Lewis Carroll's Alice, should believe "as many as six impossible things before breakfast."[1] There is no difficulty in identifying many who feel this way. While navigating that international superhighway of human knowledge and wisdom called the Internet, I came across the site www.religionisbullshit.com, making some quite strident comments on the matter, in which the words "illogical" and "irrational" featured prominently.

Common Anxieties about the Trinity

Here I want to explore this deep sense of unease that many have concerning the coherence of the doctrine of the Trinity, and how it casts light on both the theological enterprise and the issues we face in addressing our cultural situation. I begin by teasing out some aspects of the "irrationality" of the doctrine of the Trinity. Above all others, this doctrine provides us with a prism through which we may understand the traditions and tasks of Christian theology, as well as highlighting some concerns about recent directions that it has taken. To begin, I focus on issues of rationality.

The first point is obvious and rather well-worn but nevertheless merits constant repetition. There are limits to what we can understand. The first and most inconvenient of all theological responsibilities is to recognize our limitations. We can explore these at three different levels: human finitude, human creatureliness, and human sinfulness. In each of these respects, we are highlighting an aspect of our existence as finite, fallen creatures. This condition is laden with implications for our competence as thinkers and actors, and above all for our thinking and acting in relation to God. We can see this in relation to both revelation and salvation, two leading themes of Christian theology that affirm our incapacity to describe and encounter God under conditions of our own choosing, and in terms that we have determined in advance. Rationalism is epistemic Pelagianism. The first point to make, therefore, is that we must expect that our frail, sinful, and limited human capacity to reason will be severely tested when trying to accommodate itself to the divine reality. Indeed, many leading Christian theologians—and I mention Origen, Erasmus of Rotterdam, and John Calvin as obvious examples—point out that God accommodates himself to our weakness in revelation.

A second point would be that, in the relatively recent past, it was customary to excoriate the doctrine of the Trinity as irrational nonsense. If Christianity was not capable of stating its thinking about God in ways that resonated with common sense, thinking people need not take it seriously. Yet as the Enlightenment vision of human reason's scope relentlessly loses credibility, that erosion diminishes the force of this complaint to a near vanishing point. Even the notion of "common sense" is now regarded as socially constructed. As Alasdair MacIntyre explained in his *Three Rival Versions of Moral Enquiry*, philosophy in general and ethics in particular cannot proceed by means of reasoning from neutral, self-evident facts accepted by all rational persons. He concedes that many intellectuals of the late Victorian period believed exactly that, confusing the customs of their time with universal truths. However, we simply cannot sustain this view. Nearly everything philosophers have proposed as a "universal category," immune from the irritations of historical specificity, has found itself beached and shipwrecked.[2]

MacIntyre's contention that the Enlightenment proposed a theoretical criterion of justification that no one could meet in practice is of fundamental importance to the theological task. What the Enlightenment theoretically proposed no one could put into practice. People gradually realized that this massive tension between theory and practice represented more than an irritating anomaly that a later generation would sort out. It was the fatal flaw of the Enlightenment project as a whole. The Enlightenment insisted that whether something could be understood and rationally justified determined its credibility. But then the Enlightenment found itself in the rather tiresome position of having to acknowledge that it was just as "particularist" as the positions it believed it could critique from the Olympian heights, far above the specifics of history and culture.

My third point takes us off in a slightly different direction and builds once more upon growing impatience with the overstatements of the Enlightenment. One of the more troubling aspects of the Enlightenment agenda is its desire to dominate. To understand something is essential before it can be mastered. Understanding is the first step in a process of bringing something or someone to submission.

On Failing to Master God

In one sense the doctrine of the Trinity is our admission—as beings created and finite, fallen and flawed—that we simply cannot fully grasp all that God is. Was not Augustine right when he pointed to the limitations placed on our capacities, and their devastating impact on the theological enterprise? *Si comprehendis, non est Deus*.[3] One human response to this has been to argue that, since we cannot possibly grasp the mystery of God, we might as well content ourselves by creating something rather more manageable. The human desire to understand is interlocked with the darker desire to dominate. Those of us who have wrestled with the ideological program of modernity are uncomfortably aware of what Bruno Latour describes as "the double task of domination and emancipation."[4] If we are to master something, such as the natural world, we must first understand it. What Augustine termed the "eros of the mind"—meaning the sheer ecstatic delight of knowledge for its own sake—thus easily decays and degenerates into something rather more sinister. Knowledge is acquired, not to delight in the Other, but to dominate it, forcing it to serve our needs and our ends.

The doctrine of the Trinity represents a chastened admission that we are unable to master God. As Thomas Aquinas pointed out in the thirteenth century, the theologian who tries to master God is rather in the position of Jacob wrestling with the angel at Peniel (Gen. 32:24); the theologian emerges from the event bruised and defeated, yet the wiser and better for the engagement. For Augustine, to "comprehend" was to intellectually subjugate something, to proclaim the victory of the human intellect over all that it surveys. Yet Augustine was quite clear: we simply cannot "comprehend" God.

Writers sympathetic to the goals of the Enlightenment protest that such theological strategies are simply retreats into irrationalism. Yet it is important to pause and adjudicate this claim. The Enlightenment used the term "rational" in a triumphalist sense, often with a hidden meaning. Rational means what reason can account for, thus validating its own claim to mastery and autonomy. By designating what it could not master as "irrational," the Enlightenment sought to deflect attention from those aspects of reality—including the vision of God—that were clearly too much for human reason to cope with. Those areas of reality that reason could not conquer were not declared to lie *beyond* reason, but to be *contrary* to reason.

The Enlightenment now lies behind us, leaving us stranded as we seek to secure adequate criteria for knowledge, as opposed to mere opinion. With the long, lingering death of the cult of reason has come the rebirth of interest in the concept of mystery, understood in its proper sense as a matter of intellectual immensity, which our frail and finite human minds simply cannot grasp in its totality. In short, we are confronted with a mystery.

Reclaiming the Notion of "Mystery"

This brings me to my final point concerning the Trinity and rationality: the recent revalidation of the concept of *mystery*. On a Christian reading of the world, the coherence of reality is not something that is optimistically and improperly *imposed* upon a formless or inchoate actuality, but something that can be *discerned*, within the limits of our capacities as created beings. The Christian vision of things affirms the ultimate coherence of reality, so that we can hold the occasional opacity of things to reflect a mystery rather than an incoherence. Perceptions of incoherence are thus to be understood as noetic, rather than ontic, as resting on our limited capacity to perceive and to represent, rather than on the way things actually are.

Faced with a mystery, in the proper sense of the term, human beings tend to take one of two approaches: First, they may declare it to be an incoherence, which therefore need not detain us, save as offering a textbook example of primitive or superstitious beliefs, which the modernist enterprise worked so hard to eliminate. Second, they may reduce it to something more manageable, arguing that while the totality of the mystery may lie beyond us, we may be able to grasp at least some of its aspects. While both of these strategies are understandable, they are theologically problematic.

The doctrine of the Trinity gathers together the richness of the complex Christian understanding of God; it yields a vision of God to which the only appropriate response is adoration and devotion. The doctrine knits together into a coherent whole the Christian doctrines of creation, redemption, and sanctification. By doing so, it sets before us a vision of a God who created the world, whose glory can be seen reflected in the wonders of the natural order; a God who redeemed the world, whose love can be seen in the tender face of Christ; and a God who is present now in the lives of believers.

In this sense, we can reckon the doctrine to "preserve the mystery" of God, in the sense of ensuring that the Christian understanding of God is not impoverished through reductionism or rationalism. The Brazilian liberation theologian Leonardo Boff also makes this point:

> Seeing mystery in this perspective enables us to understand how it provokes reverence, the only possible attitude to what is supreme and final in our lives. Instead of strangling reason, it invites expansion of the mind and heart. It is not a mystery that leaves us dumb and terrified, but one that leaves us happy, singing and giving thanks. It is not a wall placed in front of us, but a doorway through which we go to the infinity of God. Mystery is like a cliff: we may not be able to scale it, but we can stand at the foot of it, touch it, praise its beauty. So it is with the mystery of the Trinity.[5]

So how do we wrestle with a mystery? I will offer two pointers, one drawn from the Reformation, the other from the twentieth century. One of the central themes of Martin Luther's "theology of the cross" is that we are to regard the cross as a *mystery*.[6] By this, Luther means that human reason is incapable of fully grasping the doctrine, which it therefore seeks to restate on its own terms. We can never hope to give a full account of the cross; although we can certainly delineate its many revelational, soteriological, and spiritual aspects, we cannot hope fully to plumb the depths of its meaning. Luther does not see this as a problem; it is simply the way things are, involving a chastened and responsible admission on the part of human theologians that they are not divine. The human mind's creaturely and fallen status limits it. What we can know about God we can indeed know reliably; yet we cannot fully know God.

Here Luther is stating the principle of "reserve," a leading theme in both the Cappadocian fathers and in more recent writers, such as John Henry Newman. God gives human intellect and reason, which are not contrary to revelation; yet they cannot apprehend all the mysteries of faith and must learn to accept the limitations under which they are obliged to operate.

In the twentieth century, Hans Urs von Balthasar develops a related line of thought. Von Balthasar insists upon the "totality" of the divine revelation, holding that it necessarily exceeds human comprehension. To develop this idea, he draws on the notion of *Gestalt*, a term used by Christian von Ehrenfels (1859–1932), the Austrian founder of Gestalt theory, to designate complex wholes that simply cannot be reduced to their constituent components. We are to see the whole as *more than*, and *other than*, the sum of its individual parts.[7] Von Balthasar applies such insights to the notion of revelation, which he insists is ultimately irreducible.[8]

Conceding the human need and impulse to "dissect" such a *Gestalt*, von Balthasar argues that this represents an attempt to "master" revelation,[9] and hence to subjugate it. Beholding the *Gestalt* as a totality forces us to concede the inadequacy of our fragmented approaches to mystery. We cannot hope to see *behind* the mystery; we must look for meaning *within* it, accepting the limitations on comprehension and representation that this entails.

We can understand the point at issue by considering the famous distinction Gabriel Marcel (1889–1973) developed between "problems" and "mysteries."[10] Marcel sees reality as existing on two levels, the world of the problematical and the world of the ontological mystery. For Marcel, the world of the problematical is the domain of science, rational inquiry, and technical control. Here we define the real by what the mind can conceptualize as a problem and hence solve and represent in a mathematical formula. Reality is merely the sum total of its parts. In the world of the problematical, one therefore views human beings essentially as objects, statistics, or cases, and defines them in terms of their vital functions (biological) and their social functions; one thus considers the individual as merely a biological machine performing various social functions.

Marcel's existentialist concerns lead him to consider how we might inquire about the nature of Being. However, it proves impossible to think of "Being" as a problem that can be solved through the application of objective modes of reflection. Whereas we can think of the problematic as a realm apart from us, maintaining a convenient existential distance, questions about Being make us realize that in some intimate and perhaps perplexing way we are implicated in it. It proves impossible for us to separate the question "What is Being?" from the further and more troubling question "Who (or what) are we?" Since the question of Being always involves our own existence, Marcel argues that we cannot really speak about the *problem* of Being; we here are dealing not with a *problem* but with a *mystery*. A problem is something that we can view objectively and for which we can find a possible solution. A mystery is something that we cannot view objectively, precisely because we cannot separate ourselves from it. Ontological mystery presupposes and demands engagement and involvement on our part.

Austin Farrer developed Marcel's ideas in a more explicitly theological manner in his 1948 Bampton Lectures, *The Glass of Vision*.[11] Farrer defines the realm of the problematic as "the field in which there are right answers." When we treat reality as a "problem," we "approach the world with a fixed measuring instrument, whether of the literal and physical, or of the conceptual sort." The realm of mystery, however, involves engagement with reality at such a level that we cannot investigate it in terms of "determinate and soluble problems."

Farrer illustrates this distinction, not entirely successfully, using the illustration of a yardstick, a measuring rod. He defines the reality of the problematic in terms of what we can measure.[12]

When I approach my environment, yardstick in hand, I do not ask the general question "What have we here?" or even "What here is most important?" but always the narrow question "What will my yardstick tell me about the things that are here?" We justly credit the true scientist with a supreme respect for fact, for the real world upon which he makes his experiments. The scientist will stubbornly refuse to record what his yardstick does not bring to light.

Here Farrer's concern is to emphasize that the realm of what may be measured leads on into another, deeper realm: the realm of the metaphysical.[13] Where the attitude of almost passive respect combines with a rigorous demand for understanding, metaphysical activity will appear. Since the metaphysician has no already-formulated tests to apply, and no yardstick to presuppose, no determinate and soluble problems arise for him: there are no "right answers" to his inquiries. He does not face the limited and manageable relation that arises between a conceptual instrument and the object it is applied to. Instead, he faces the object itself, in all its fullness, and the object meets him not as a cluster of problems but as a single though manifold mystery.

Each of these mysteries is distinct and unique, which we must approach and understand in terms of its own identity, even if some common metaphysical tools—such as the use of analogies—may prove helpful in reaching an understanding of each mystery.[14]

The analysis that Marcel and Farrer present points to the perennial nature of the theological task: duty calls each generation to wrestle with mystery, knowing that it possesses a certain inexhaustibility that any one writer or era cannot exhaust. Although we may see a problem as an intellectual difficulty that we can resolve through abstract, analytical, and objective reflection, a mystery remains alive and interesting no matter how successfully one has dealt with it in previous attempts. The problematical is the domain of science and rational inquiry. Once we solve a problem, we may have no more interest in it. A mystery, however, challenges, refreshes, and reinvigorates the theological task, not least through the expectation that fresh light has yet to break forth from mysteries that previous generations have wrestled with.

The process of wrestling with a mystery thus remains open, not closed. What one generation inherits from another are not so much definitive answers as shared commitments to the process of wrestling. Christian theology has long recognized this insight. Traditionally, Christian doctrine has been well aware of its limits and has sought to avoid excessively confident affirmations in the face of mystery. Yet at the same time, Christian theology has never seen itself as totally reduced to silence in the face of divine mysteries. Charles Gore rightly insisted:

> Human language never can express adequately divine realities. A constant tendency to apologize for human speech, a great element of agnosticism, an awful sense of unfathomed depths beyond the little that is made known, is always present to the mind of theologians who know what they are about, in conceiving or expressing God. "We see," says St Paul, "in a mirror, in terms of a riddle;" "we know in part." "We are compelled," complains St Hilary, "to attempt what is unattainable, to climb where we cannot reach, to speak what we cannot utter; instead of the mere adoration of faith, we are compelled to entrust the deep things of religion to the perils of human expression."[15]

Thus far I have been exploring how the doctrine of the Trinity encourages us to reflect long and hard on our capacities as thinkers. For Karl Barth, as many of you know, the very fact that we know *anything* about God rests on divine self-revelation, and the actuality of that revelation is firmly grounded in a trinitarian vision of God. To "know God" and to "know God as Trinity" are thus intimately interconnected. The twentieth-century rediscovery of the doctrine of the Trinity, due in no small part to Barth's massive contribution in this field, has thus brought some welcome advantages.

Nevertheless, here I want to introduce a note of caution. Has the trinitarian pendulum swung too far? Has a legitimate correction become an overcorrection? Has an entirely justified concern to restore a biblically warranted and theologically appropriate way of thinking about God itself become prone to overstatement? In the rest of this essay, I explore two fundamental concerns about recent trends in trinitarian thinking. These concerns reflect my own particular emphases as an evangelical, especially my concern to remain as close as possible to the language and conceptualities of Scripture. Nevertheless, these concerns go beyond an evangelical constituency and represent genuine problems in current trinitarian thought. I can sum up my concerns under two broad categories. First, I am concerned that much trinitarian theological reflection has lost its moorings in Scripture. Second, I wish to raise the question of whether one can speak of the doctrine of the Trinity as playing a foundational role in theology, when it is, in my view, something that we infer from other foundations. I hope that both these concerns will become clearer as I proceed.

Evangelicalism and the Doctrine of the Trinity

I observe that most evangelicals do not seem to consider explicit engagement with the doctrine of the Trinity to be of major importance. By this I do not mean that evangelicals have ignored the doctrine. Major evangelical surveys of Christian theology routinely engage with the doctrine; more recent discussions have addressed such contemporary issues as whether the generally masculine language used to articulate the doctrine causes difficulties. My point is somewhat different. Let me illustrate this by exploring the role played by the doctrine in the writings of John R. W. Stott, widely regarded as one of the most important British evangelical theologians of the twentieth century. At no point does Stott treat the doctrine at length, although one could argue that the doctrine is implicit in much of his more academic writings.

Stott's use of the Trinity is particularly illuminating. Positively, he regards it as the basis of an evangelical understanding of the Bible: "The Bible is the witness of the Father to the Son through the Holy Spirit."[16] Negatively, he treats it as a difficulty that we must overcome in discussions with Judaism and Islam, which can misunderstand it as compromising the unity of God.[17] In general, while affirming the Trinity, Stott tends to stress that the Christian faith is Christ-centered and cites the disproportion of the clauses in the Apostles' Creed as an illustration of this point.[18]

So what are we to infer from this observation? In discussion with colleagues, two possible (and I must add, potentially complementary) reasons emerge. First, there is the desire to remain as faithful as possible to both the language and conceptualities of Scripture. Evangelicalism has always valued proximity to Scripture. The history of the movement has shown that its best theologians are those who prize an active, reflective engagement with Scripture as an integral aspect of the theological task. Evangelicalism has a number of ways of conceptualizing both its identity[19] and its approach to theologizing—if I might be allowed this verbal form, which stresses that theology is an *activity*. Nevertheless, I insist that one of the most fundamental and essential distinctives of the evangelical approach to theology is its insistence that we must nourish and govern theology at all points by Holy Scripture, and seek to offer a faithful and coherent account of what it finds there.

This means that evangelicalism aims to keep as close as possible to the conceptualities and vocabulary of Scripture. We can see an excellent example of this concern in recent evangelical discussion of the term "spirituality," which is increasingly being accepted within the evangelical constituency. Yet a concern that many expressed at an earlier stage in this discussion was that "spirituality" is a nonbiblical term. I think it is fair to say that evangelicals now accept that such terms may be used; after all, the term "theology" itself falls into this category of nonbiblical terms. But we see the desire to remain close to the vocabulary of Scripture as being important, and I believe this concern is justified.

In this trend I see much that resonates with the theological method of the patristic period. I recognize, for example, the enormous reluctance of many patristic writers to go beyond the ideas or vocabulary of Scripture, except when the sheer force of the biblical witness itself clearly obligates them to do so. Thus, Athanasius's commendation of the nonbiblical term *homoousios* (of the same substance) was clearly shaped by two concerns: Christians were reluctant to use such a clearly unbiblical term. They also believed that it was necessary for Christians to use a nonbiblical term to ensure that they properly articulated and defended some fundamentally biblical concepts.

I firmly believe that Scripture legitimates a doctrine of the Trinity.[20] The history of debating this issue bears out that this is not self-evidently true, especially in tracing the rise of evangelical antitrinitarianism in more radical reforming circles of the sixteenth century. The argument here was very simple: the word "biblical" means "what is explicitly revealed in Scripture." Since the Scripture does not reveal the doctrine of the Trinity in this manner, there is no obligation for any evangelical to accept it. I recognize merit in that concern; my response is to argue that the term "biblical" extends to include ideas that Scripture does not explicitly state, but which we may reasonably infer from what it does state. I do not see this as problematic; indeed, the history of biblical interpretation within the early church cautiously proceeded in three stages and was essentially complete by the end of the fourth century.

> Stage 1: Recognizing the full divinity of Jesus Christ.
> Stage 2: Recognizing the full divinity of the Spirit.
> Stage 3: Definitively formulating the doctrine of the Trinity, embedding and clarifying these central insights, and determining their mutual relationship.

Like Luther and Calvin, I see the doctrine of the Trinity as a biblically warranted doctrine. But this is not quite the same as saying that it is a doctrine Scripture itself explicitly reveals. I refer to a foundational document of Anglicanism, the Thirty-Nine Articles of Religion (1563). The sixth of these articles runs as follows:

> Holy Scripture containeth all things necessary to salvation: so that whatsoever is not read therein, nor may be proved thereby, is not to be required of any man, that it should be believed as an article of the faith, or be thought requisite or necessary to salvation.

This article draws a clear distinction between "what is read therein" and "what may be proved thereby." The doctrine of the Trinity belongs to the latter category rather than to the former: it may be proved by Scripture.

The second reason scholars offer for evangelicals' reluctance to make much use of the doctrine of the Trinity is that many sections of evangelicalism are thoroughly populist in their orientation. Thus they adopt a principled refusal to become involved in abstract or complex theological debates.[21] They see these as distancing the movement from its grass roots. I have no intention of criticizing this trend. One of the reasons why evangelicalism has proved to be so successful is that it remains faithful and sensitive to the needs, concerns, and modes of discourse and conceptualization of ordinary people. The doctrine of the Trinity, and more specifically its arcane vocabulary, often seems a million miles away from the everyday world of middle America.

Yet I need to express a legitimate concern. The popular language of faith is somewhat removed from that of technical theological discussions. Evangelicals gladly end their meetings by saying the "grace"; they do so, however, primarily because it is a biblical citation. They have no difficulty in conceding that we can discern a trinitarian substructure within the language of popular piety. But why, many ask, do we need to do anything other than acknowledge that this is the case while continuing to use this language? I can easily argue that the simple slogan of faith "Jesus saves!" has an implicit trinitarian foundation. But does that mean that I cease saying "Jesus saves!" or that I feel impelled to add a rather long—and I suspect somewhat cumbersome—trinitarian footnote to this simple affirmation?

The Danger of Trinitarian Inflation

So where does this line of thought take us? I think it leads us to two conclusions. First, it warns against the dangers of inflationary trinitarian language and speculation, which has lost its moorings in the language of Scripture. I make this point particularly in response to some more recent theological exaggerations and posturings. These have, sadly, emerged from an overzealous and perhaps rather uncritical reading of the notion of the *imago Dei*, as some link it with the doctrine of the Trinity and produce a syllogism along the following lines:

God, as Trinity, is X.
Humanity is created in the image of God.
Therefore, humanity is also X.

The doctrine of the Trinity seems to be singularly ill suited to functioning as a criterion or point of access to other theological insights in this manner. From an evangelical perspective, this tendency is especially disturbing: it marks a serious erosion of any willingness to be closely attentive to the biblical text, heading off into what Luther and Calvin would regard as the less impressive type of scholastic speculation. The new vocabulary that has emerged from this style of theological speculation may be regarded as illustrating precisely the kind of unanchored speculation that a responsible theology aims to discourage.

Second, this line of thought reminds us of the need to ensure a connection between the language of the theological academy and that of the community of faith. One of the real difficulties is that of communicating the doctrine of the Trinity: how do we explain to a sympathetic and receptive audience that we need to use this apparently cumbersome and perplexing way of speaking about God?

My main concern, however, lies in the ease with which trinitarian speculation can lose its rooting in Scripture and fly off into the theological stratosphere. Let me stress that this kind of speculation may be interesting and enjoyable, and that I have no objection to people doing it in private. But when this passes into the public language of the church, things can begin to go wrong. I illustrate this by considering social approaches to the Trinity.[22] Writers such as Leonardo Boff and others have developed the idea that the Trinity models a "divine society," which can serve as the basis, exemplar, or inspiration for the church in particular and society in general.[23] As Thomas Parker puts it:

> The political meaning of the doctrine of the Trinity comes as an invitation to share in the struggle for that form of human community which expresses the truth symbolized in God the blessed Trinity. . . . The one whose unity is a living out of difference, and whose being is in communion with creatures is no sanction for oppression, violence, injustice or tyranny.[24]

Here Parker sees the relation of Father, Son, and Spirit as a model for social existence in the world. Doubtless there is some truth in this, and I have no wish to challenge the idea that reflection on the nature and character of God can be an important stimulus and foundation for church and society. My concern is how this process of reflection takes place.

The process of argumentation leading to such an application of the doctrine of the Trinity smuggles in ideological ideas, which subsequently find their expression in its social application. Reading works such as Jürgen Moltmann's *Trinity and the Kingdom of God* often leaves one with a sense of bafflement at how he can adduce a series of rather ambitious social and communitarian doctrines from the mystery of the Trinity.[25] It is all quite well to speak about the church as an "icon of the Trinity."[26] But how can we ground a concrete reality in a theological abstraction that itself is the outcome of theological reflection on divine revelation? Are we not in danger of giving normative status to covert assumptions that have found their way into the process of theological reasoning, in effect proceeding from hidden cultural presuppositions to explicit theological applications without the application of due critical reflection?

Perhaps I have overstated my anxiety at this point. My concern is that the theological pendulum has swung excessively in a trinitarian direction, so that one is thought negligent if one does not invoke the doctrine in theological reflection. I fully concede the need to recover this doctrine from the dark night of the so-called Enlightenment; and I applaud writers—such as Barth, Rahner, Gunton, and Jenson—who have helped us do this. But reactions often overcompensate in response to perceived deficiencies. I simply ask whether we are now seeing an outbreak of theological nonsense that may actually discredit the doctrine of the Trinity and hasten our return to the deistic modes of thought our forebears favored. My plea is for a trinitarian modesty.

Visualizing the Trinity

I now turn to my final point. The real difficulty for most people lies in the *visualization* of the Trinity. How can we make sense of such a complex and abstract idea? Patrick, the patron saint of Ireland, is rumored to have used the leaf of a shamrock to illustrate how a single leaf could have three different elements. In his letters Gregory of Nyssa uses a series of analogies to help his readers grasp the reality of the Trinity, including these:[27]

- The analogy of a spring, fount, and stream of water. The one flows from the other, and they share the same substance— water. Although we may distinguish different aspects of the stream of water, we cannot separate them.
- The analogy of a chain. There are many links in a chain; yet being connected to one means being connected to all

of them. In the same way, Gregory argues, someone who encounters the Holy Spirit also encounters the Father and the Son.

- The analogy of a rainbow. Drawing on the Nicene statement that Christ is "Light from Light," Gregory argues that the rainbow allows us to distinguish and appreciate the different colors of a sunbeam. There is only one beam of light, and yet the colors blend seamlessly into one another.

In what follows, we explore one more recent way of thinking about the Trinity that has proved quite helpful to many. We associate it with the contemporary American Lutheran theologian Robert Jenson, who sets it out in his work *The Triune Identity: God according to the Gospel*.[28]

In this work Jenson argues that "Father, Son, and Holy Spirit" is the proper name for the God whom Christians know in and through Jesus Christ. It is imperative, he maintains, that God should have a proper name. "Trinitarian discourse is Christianity's effort to identify the God who has claimed us. The doctrine of the Trinity comprises both a proper name, 'Father, Son and Holy Spirit,' . . . and an elaborate development and analysis of corresponding identifying descriptions." Jenson points out that ancient Israel lived in a polytheistic context, in which the term "god" conveyed relatively little information. It was necessary to *name* the god in question. The writers of the New Testament confronted a similar situation; they needed to identify the God at the heart of their faith and distinguish this God from the many other gods worshipped and acknowledged in the region, especially in Asia Minor.

The doctrine of the Trinity thus *identifies* and *names* the Christian God, but identifies and names this God in a manner consistent with the biblical witness. It is not a name that we have chosen; it is a name that has been chosen for us, which we are authorized to use. In this way Jenson defends the priority of God's self-revelation against human constructions of concepts of divinity. "The gospel identifies its God thus: God is the one who raised Israel's Jesus from the dead. The whole task of theology can be described as the unpacking of this sentence in various ways. One of these produces the church's trinitarian language and thought." The doctrine of the Trinity, Jenson affirms, allows the church to discover the distinctiveness of its creed and thus avoid becoming absorbed by rival conceptions of God.

Hence, the doctrine of the Trinity centers on the recognition that Scripture and the witness of the church do name God. Within the Hebraic tradition, historical events identify God. Jenson recognizes how many Old Testament texts identify God with reference to divine acts in history, such as the liberation of Israel from its captivity in Egypt. The same pattern is evident in the New Testament, which identifies God with reference to specific historical events, supremely in the resurrection of Jesus Christ. The text identifies God in relation to Jesus Christ. Who is God? Which god are we talking about? The God who raised Christ from the dead. As Jenson puts it, "The emergence of a semantic pattern in which the uses of 'God' and 'Jesus Christ' are mutually determining" is of fundamental importance within the New Testament.

The gospel of the New Testament provides a new identifying description for this God, the same as the God of Israel. The event, to which the whole New Testament witnesses, begins to apply this new description. In the gospel, God is "whoever raised Jesus from the dead." Identification of God by the resurrection did not replace identification by the exodus; it is essential to the God who raised Jesus that he is the same one who freed Israel. But the new thing that is the content of the gospel is that God has now identified himself also as "him who raised Jesus our Lord from the dead" (Rom. 4:24). In the New Testament such phrases become the standard way of referring to God.

Jenson thus recovers a personal conception of God from metaphysical speculation. "Father, Son, and Holy Spirit" is a proper name, which the church asks us to use in naming and addressing God. "Linguistic means of identification—proper names, identifying descriptions, or both—are a necessity of religion. Prayers, like other requests and praises, must be addressed." The Trinity is thus an instrument of theological precision, which forces us to be explicit about the God under discussion. Christians do not believe in a generic god, but in a very specific God who is known in and through a series of actions in history.

I end, however, with a dose of theological cold water, something that will, I trust, help us to keep a sense of perspective in all our thinking and doing as we reflect on this doctrine and its

implications for Christian life and thought. During the Middle
Ages the theology of the Trinity became the subject of consid-
erable theological speculation, occasionally leading people to
see the Trinity as little more than a mathematical puzzle or
logical riddle. Thomas à Kempis (c. 1380–1471) vigorously opposed this trend, seeing the proper role of theology as leading to
love for God, contrition, and a changed life. In his *Imitation of
Christ*, Thomas sets out a strongly antispeculative approach to
the Christian faith, which rests firmly on the need to obey Christ
rather than to indulge in flights of intellectual fancy. Thomas
even singles out speculation concerning the Trinity as something
to avoid—unless it transforms us.

> What good does it do one to dispute loftily about the Trinity, but
> lack humility and therefore displease the Trinity? It is not lofty
> words that make a person righteous or holy or dear to God, but
> a virtuous life.[29]

And with that note of caution, I end!

2

Out of the Box

The Christian Experience of God in Trinity

GERALD L. BRAY

Because you are sons, God has sent the Spirit of his Son into our hearts, crying: "Abba! Father!"

Galatians 4:6 ESV

Introduction

Why did a new religion arise out of the life and teachings of Jesus of Nazareth? We may dispute the precise details, but we cannot doubt that, sometime around the middle of the first Christian century, the followers of Jesus had formed a community of faith that was distinct from its Jewish parent, and that Jews who remained unconvinced by this community's claims about Jesus regarded its members with hostility. Since the first Christians were themselves Jews, and often Jews of a particularly observant kind, what can explain their apparent willingness to abandon their fellow countrymen and coreligionists in order to make common cause with non-Jewish people who believed in Christ? Was Christianity not just a form of Judaism, albeit with a somewhat eccentric take on the Law and the Prophets?

If this indeed had been the case, it is unlikely that the Christian church would ever have broken with its parent body as quickly or as completely as it did. Judaism had already developed a sectarian fringe, and the Samaritans had produced a variant form that, though greatly detested by orthodox Jews, was nevertheless part of the Jewish world in a way that pagan cults were not. Christianity, however, was different, though in a way that was not immediately clear. It was not a Jewish sect, like that of the Essenes, nor was it an aberrant form of Judaism, like Samaritanism. It appealed to non-Jews, or Gentiles, but it was not pagan, nor could one reasonably regard it as a syncretistic mixture of Judaism and some form of Gentile religious belief. What then was it?

The apostle Paul originally wrote Galatians 4:6 in the heat of a controversy concerning the relationship of the Jewish law to the Christian gospel, and we should not underestimate its significance. A little reflection on its meaning will show that it is of central importance for understanding why Christianity became a new religion, derived from the same sources as Judaism, but essentially independent of it. Paul wrote his letter to the Galatians around 49, which makes it one of the earliest books in our New Testament (possibly the earliest).

Hardly anyone questions its authenticity, and the context of this vitally important verse makes it clear that some later hand cannot have added it as a gloss. It forms an integral part of Paul's argument, and by all the normal canons of literary judgment, we must conclude that here we are dealing with the apostle's own words and his deepest convictions. Furthermore, he was writing primarily to non-Jewish believers, to explain to them why they had no need to become Jews in order to be good Christians, despite Christianity's close links with Judaism. Hence, to interpret this verse from that perspective is consonant with the overall thrust of the letter. Paul had no desire to diminish the importance of the Old Testament, nor did he wish to deny the special place that the Jewish people—his own nation—occupied in the cosmic plan of divine redemption. He knew perfectly well that one could not understand the message of Christ apart from Judaism, or without constant reference to it, and for that reason he always maintained that, because of their background and early religious training, Jewish Christians had an advantage over Gentiles.

But at the same time, Paul also insisted that people could not equate the Christian gospel with Judaism or subsume the gospel into Judaism. He was convinced that the coming of Christ had brought something new into the world, which traditional Judaism could not absorb. To use a biblical metaphor, the new wine of his gospel had burst the old wineskin of the Mosaic covenant, the basic framework within which religious leaders had conceived the Judaism of his day (cf. Matt. 9:17). However much we might continue to respect and admire that wineskin, Paul argued, since the coming of Christ into the world, it can no longer serve as an adequate framework for expressing our relationship to God.

In saying this, the apostle was not theorizing about some abstract theological idea. On the contrary, he was describing to his readers what he regarded as an experience that they both already shared, and he expected it to resonate as such with them. From the beginning, the Christian knowledge of God in Trinity was first experiential and later theoretical, an order of things that has always characterized authentic Christian understanding and confession. We may even say that whenever theory has claimed pride of place over experience, the result has been some form of heresy, as for example in the Arian controversies of the fourth and fifth centuries. Arius wanted to make sense of God, and so he dissolved the Trinity into a hierarchy of beings, the last two of which were creatures and therefore ontologically inferior to the first. But the living experience of the worshipping community broke the bonds that Arius's philosophical logic would have imposed on its faith. In the process, that experience reshaped human thought and language into a vehicle capable of expressing a mystery that unaided human reason was (and is) unable to grasp. In a quite real sense, therefore, we can expound the Christian doctrine of the Trinity as an extended commentary on the meaning of this verse in Galatians, which not only reflects the earliest stage of the Christian message but also defines the most characteristic feature of that message.

The Link with Judaism

To understand what the apostle Paul was getting at, we need to look first at the links that tied his faith in Christ to his inherited Judaism. I cannot stress too strongly that Paul never regarded his Christian conversion as a repudiation of his Jewish inheritance. As he says in the preceding two verses (Gal. 4:4–5), Jesus Christ came to the Jewish people and ministered almost exclusively to them. His message was one that only Jews could fully understand, and he clearly wanted them to accept it as the true interpretation of their ancient Scriptures. At no point did either Jesus or Paul make any attempt to deny or reinterpret the ancient revelation of the One God to the nation of Israel. The church consistently rejected as heretical the subsequent efforts by Marcion, the Gnostics, and others to drive a wedge between an Old Testament creator and a New Testament redeemer. However God meant for the Israelites to understand the law of Moses, Jesus and Paul took it to be the word of the same God whom Christians worship as a Trinity of persons, and the church has always accepted that witness to the divine unity.

Yet Jesus Christ had proclaimed a new revelation that did not merely add to the old. It also forced those who accepted it to look at their Old Testament inheritance in a new light.

Paul's argument, like that of the early church in general, was not a challenge to Judaism from the outside, but a new hermeneutic, which the Christians wanted to apply to sacred texts that they shared in common with the Jews. The basic contention of this new hermeneutic was that the historic covenant between God and the Jews went back several centuries before Moses, and derived ultimately from Abraham. It was to Abraham that God had first revealed himself, and because Abraham had believed God's promises to him, God had originally established a special relationship between himself and Abraham. In other words, the covenant embodied in the law of Moses was based on an unwritten experience of God that both predated that law and determined what its parameters would be. By applying this hermeneutic, Christians claimed that knowledge of God depended not on obedience to the commands of the Mosaic law, which were of secondary importance, but on a special relationship with God, exemplified by Abraham, which was received and maintained by faith, or trust in his promises. This relationship with God also involved obedience, but it was obedience of a different character from that demanded by the law. To use Paul's language, the obedience of faith is that of a son in his father's household, whereas the obedience of the law is that of a servant in his master's domain. Christians and Jews shared many names for God, but only Christians prayed to him as their Father, an approach revealing the nature of their new covenant, which they adopted because Jesus had taught them to do so in imitation of himself.

Hence, there is a sense in which we can trace a distinctively Christian understanding of God right back to the prayer that Jesus taught his disciples: "Our Father in heaven, hallowed be your name" (Matt. 6:9). Calling God "Father" (or "Abba" in Aramaic), was one of the most characteristic features of Jesus's teaching, and it is no accident that Paul picked up on it in Galatians 4:6. Though father language for God is not entirely absent from the piety of the Old Testament, as we shall see, most Jews were unused to it, and at least some of them felt uncomfortable when they heard Jesus using it, not least because by calling God his Father, Jesus appeared to be making himself God's equal (John 5:18).

In other respects, though, it is safe to say that, apart from Marcion and the Gnostics, the early Christians accepted everything that Judaism taught them about the nature of God. No orthodox Christian ever questioned God's eternity, invisibility, omnipotence, omniscience, or absolute uniqueness. For them, as for Jews, there was only one God in heaven and earth, the One who had revealed himself to the Jewish patriarchs as Yahweh, a name that the ancient Hebrews understood to mean "He who is" (cf. Exod. 3:14). Later, when Judaism came into contact with ancient Greek culture, that understanding made it possible for both Jews and Christians to equate the biblical God with the Supreme Being of the Greek philosophical schools. That equation permitted them to engage in dialogue with their philosophies in ways that would leave a deep mark on later Christian theology. But it is significant that no one made an attempt to identify Yahweh with an Olympian deity like Zeus (Jupiter), probably because the Olympian gods were neither unique nor omnipotent. Perhaps the Romans thought he was Saturn, but if so, that was

only because Jews worshipped him on Saturn's day, and no Jewish or Christian writer ever adopted this rather odd idea.

The Disagreement with Judaism

The basic acceptance of Jewish theology that has always characterized the Christian church is an important link between
Judaism and Christianity, but this agreement is not unqualified.
In practice, we must admit that most of the time the differences
between the Jewish and Christian perceptions of God have mat-
tered more in the course of history, and in ancient times they
quickly led to a radical separation of the two traditions. Whatever
the personal, political, or circumstantial elements involved in
that separation may have been, they were not the decisive fac-
tors. At its root lay perceptions of God so different that Jews
and Christians no longer recognized each other as belonging
to a single community of faith. As Paul says in Galatians 4:6,
Christians claim that God has sent the Spirit of his Son into our
hearts, crying, "Abba! Father!" Spirit, Son, Father—the work of
these three characterizes the Christian experience of God in a
way that Jews regard as incompatible with their belief in the
undifferentiated One. Christians reject this, claiming instead that
the three *are* one, and one in a way that is perfectly consistent
with the Old Testament revelation! It is a belief that makes no
sense in Jewish terms, and later the Muslims rejected it as well,
for not dissimilar reasons. In the community of monotheistic
faiths, Christianity is the odd one out, trying to reconcile unity
with plurality in God for reasons that other monotheists find
incomprehensible.

Do Christians really need to do this? Can we not surrender
our particularity in this respect and join a broad offensive of
monotheistic faith in a world that officially tries to dispense with
God altogether? Since 1945, most Christians have revised their
ancient prejudices against Jews, and now they often seek to make
common cause with them on moral and cultural issues. More
recently, increasing contact with Islam has produced a similar
reaction, though admittedly on a more limited scale, at least so
far. In this kind of interfaith dialogue, the pressures on Christians to abandon trinitarianism are great; yet when the crunch

has come, the church has always refused to take that apparently easier road. More than that, for some curious reason the recent rapprochement with Judaism and the burgeoning contacts with other faiths have gone hand in hand with an astonishing revival of trinitarian theology within the church itself. A doctrine that seemed to be in retreat a generation ago has returned to center stage at the very moment when outside pressures appear to militate against it. Why is it so hard for Christians to let go of the Trinity when there seem to be so many things they may gain by doing so?

From Outside to Inside

The key to understanding this lies in appreciating the essential difference between Christianity and Judaism in the first instance, but also between Christianity and most other belief systems in the modern world. As far as Judaism is concerned, Christianity has introduced a hermeneutical shift in its interpretation of the Old Testament. One may describe the shift in simple terms as going from a perspective basically external to one that is basically internal. This is a bold statement, and one has to express and understand it with greater subtlety than it might initially seem to allow. To say that Old Testament Judaism was a religion in which external things were fundamental is not to deny the reality of an Old Testament Jewish spirituality, any more than the affirmation that Christianity is primarily an internal experience of God means that it has no meaningful outward forms of expression. What we identify here is a shift of emphasis and perspective within a framework in which both the external and the internal are necessary for the worshipper to appreciate the whole reality. Nevertheless, the difference is sufficiently important for it to have produced a new religion that cannot return to the bosom of the old without losing its essential character.

That Judaism is defined primarily by external criteria appears from the law of Moses. According to that law, the people of Israel are set apart from the nations by the rite of circumcision, which leaves a permanent, visible mark on the body, and by a whole series of statutes designed to create observable differences between Jews and other people. God gives the Israelites a specific territory in which to dwell, where their destiny will be worked out in the sight of all other nations. They are told to avoid certain types of food, to restrict close relations with non-Jews (and in particular to avoid intermarriage with them), and to concentrate their worship in the elaborate sacrificial rituals of the Jerusalem temple. In biblical Judaism, the temple was of particular importance because there God met with his people, albeit in a highly structured way. Once a year, the law allowed the high priest to enter the inner room known as the holy of holies, where he offered the sacrifice of atonement for the sins of the entire nation. Functioning in the holy place without authorization courted disaster, as King Uzziah discovered to his cost. When he tried to offer sacrifices in the temple, he was struck with leprosy—an object lesson, if ever there was one, in what was allowed and what was not (2 Chron. 26:16–21).

The temple was only the last and most sumptuous form of the space in which the meeting with God took place. Before it was constructed, there was the tabernacle, which accompanied the people in the desert. In the tabernacle lay the ark of the covenant, a sacred box containing the charter instruments of the Mosaic dispensation. The ark was strictly off-limits to the profane—so much so that when a man named Uzzah tried to prevent it from falling to the ground on its bumpy journey across the Judean countryside, he was struck dead for touching it (1 Chron. 13:10). In ancient Israel, God dwelt in the midst of his people, but people could not approach him directly, except for the few whom the law authorized to do so. To be sure, the prophet Jeremiah knew that one day God would write his law in our hearts (Jer. 31:31–34), but this was a prophecy for the future, and it is symptomatic of the difference between Judaism and Christianity that the early Christians specifically declared that it had been fulfilled in their time (Heb. 8:8–12). In fact, the more we look at the New Testament, the more we see that these symbolic markers of Judaism's restrictiveness provoked the most ardent polemic in favor of the new dispensation brought by Christ.

In that Christian dispensation, there was to be no holy land, no temple, and no ark of the covenant. The ritual of baptism, which has replaced that of circumcision, may be a visible act, but since baptism leaves no permanent mark on the body, one must regard it as essentially invisible. Like Jews, Christians are

required to be careful about the kinds of relations they enter
into with nonbelievers, and the apostle Paul still forbids intermarriage with them. But the gospel does not expect Christians
to form a distinct nation in the way that Israel was. The apostle
Paul expressed all this quite clearly only a few lines before his
trinitarian statement, declaring that in Christ the barriers between male and female, Jew and Gentile, slave and free have
been broken down (Gal. 3:28).

Christians stand in the presence of God, not because they are
the *physical* descendants of Abraham, the ancestor of Israel, but
because they are his *spiritual* descendants. Because we believe as
Abraham believed, we have received the inheritance God originally promised to him. It is also because the Jews have rejected
this understanding of the matter that they have been excluded
from God's blessing, at least for the time being. In Paul's mind, it
is not Christians who have rejected Judaism, but Jews who have
rejected Christ, and moreover, those Jews were being unfaithful to
their own heritage in so doing. Paul always believed that Israel's
faith was essentially spiritual, as was the faith of Christians, and
he regarded the Mosaic law as a kind of covering, which God
introduced in order to keep the wayward Israelites on the straight
and narrow way. Unfortunately, later generations had come to
mistake the husk for the kernel, and so they had fundamentally
misinterpreted the true meaning of the Scripture. The coming
of Christ did away with the husk, opening up the kernel to give
us direct access to God (cf. Eph. 2:18).

In the words of the Synoptic Gospels, the veil in the temple was
torn in two when Jesus was crucified, and the way into the holy
of holies was opened up (Matt. 27:51; Mark 15:38; Luke 23:45).
We who are Christians have gone into that inner sanctum, and
in Paul's words, God has now seated us in the heavenly places in
Christ Jesus (Eph. 2:6). To put it another way, whereas ordinary
Jews were kept out of the holiest place in the temple, Christians
have been admitted into the inner life of God. Only in that context, and based on that understanding, can we reconcile Christian theology with the Old Testament revelation. The God who
appears as One to those who view him on the outside, reveals
himself as a Trinity of persons, once his inner life is opened up
to our experience. The Christian doctrine that has resulted from
this is nothing more nor less than a description of what that

experience of God's inner life is like. We now turn our attention to an exploration of that inner life of God.

The Inner Life of God: The Person of the Father

In Galatians 4:6 the apostle Paul lays the groundwork for his assertion about the persons of the Trinity in a short phrase that readers often overlook. "Because you are sons," he says, God has revealed himself to us in this new and extraordinary way. The category of "sonship" as a description of our relationship with God is unique to Christianity; the early Christians used it as a mark to distinguish them from Jews, who appeared to Christians to be no more than "servants" of God. Anyone bothered by the apparent chauvinism of the term "sonship" can recognize that it is a metaphor we have to take alongside other images used in the New Testament, notably the one saying that the church is the bride of Christ (Rev. 21:2). Gender references of this kind have their place in helping us to understand the nature of our relationship with God, but they apply equally to both males and females. Every Christian is therefore in one sense a son of God and in another sense a bride of Christ, since both types of relationship reveal something of what our experience of God is like. In Galatians 4:6, Paul speaks of our "sonship" because that is the one that best describes our relationship to the Father. The bridal imagery, on the other hand, appears mainly in the eschatological context of the book of Revelation because it points to the relationship we shall enjoy with Christ when he has brought all things under his rule and summons us to reign with him in heaven.

We must consider the question of sonship at greater length, but before we do so we ought to take a closer look at the term "Father." The fatherhood of God is a concept so widely accepted in modern times that few people bother to consider what it really means. At one level, we can equate it with God's work of creation, as Paul apparently did when he preached in Athens (Acts 17:28). But it is noticeable that he quoted the pagan Greek poet Aratus when doing so, and not the Old Testament, which seldom if ever conflates these two ideas. The idea that God is *Israel's* father does occasionally occur in the Old Testament (e.g., Jer. 31:9;

Mal. 2:10), but this only occurs in contexts making it clear that the father-son imagery applies to the covenant relationship that the ancient Jews had with God. We have no evidence that it ever extended beyond this, to take in the whole of the created order. But at the same time, if the use of father-son language was possible, it was not common, and when Jesus taught his disciples to pray to God as their Father, his command came across, both to them and to others, as something fundamentally new.

Jesus clearly intended his disciples to understand the Father as the God whom they already worshipped. But is it possible to make a simple equation between the Old Testament God and the Father of Jesus Christ? To put the matter a different way, is the God of the Old Testament only the First Person of the Trinity, or is he in some sense all three combined? In Galatians 4:6, it is the undifferentiated "God" who has sent his Son's Spirit into our hearts, and from the context it appears that we must identify him with the Father, especially since the Spirit's mission is to cry "Abba" in our hearts. Furthermore, there are other New Testament examples that we might quote in support of this. For example, 2 Corinthians 13:14 says: "May the grace of our Lord Jesus Christ, and the love of God, and the fellowship of the Holy Spirit be with you all" (NIV). In the context it is clear that the "love of God" must be a reference to God the Father, and so the question naturally arises as to whether we can say that the Father is God in a way in which the Son and the Holy Spirit are not. If we can, the doctrine of the Trinity would be seriously affected and may even fall to the ground, particularly in its traditional, orthodox form, and we may find ourselves closer to Judaism than most Christians in the past have imagined.

Nevertheless, we cannot say that the God of the Old Testament is just the First Person of the Trinity without further qualification. Whatever texts like the ones quoted above might suggest, such an assertion goes against other claims that the New Testament makes for Jesus. It would take too long to elaborate on this in detail, but we can grasp the essential point by looking at the term "creator." In the opening chapters of Genesis, God appears in this role, and the theme recurs periodically throughout the Hebrew Bible. But the New Testament also says that the Son has been the creator of the world (John 1:3; Col. 1:16), so that to identify the Creator only with the First Person of the

Godhead is a form of reductionism that betrays the witness of the New Testament. We must not forget that Jesus claimed to be the uniquely complete revelation of God the Father (John 14:7), and that later the apostle Paul would tell the Colossians that in him the fullness of the Godhead dwelt bodily (Col. 2:9). If it is really true, as Jesus told his disciples, that no one can come to the Father except through him (John 14:6), then it must follow that the ancient Jews could not have known God apart from Christ, even though the latter was hidden from their eyes at the time. The Old Testament God must therefore be more than just the Father, even though various parts of the New Testament seem to equate the two. How can we account for this?

The answer to this question seems to lie in the assertion, often made in the course of church history but frequently denied in modern times, that the Father is in some sense the "anchor" person in the Trinity. We may express the traditional view by saying that whereas the Son is the person who became incarnate in Jesus Christ, and the Holy Spirit is the person who dwells in our hearts by faith, the Father is the person who primarily manifests what we now call "divinity." He is the reminder that however much God comes to us and reveals himself to us, he remains in a fundamental sense hidden from our eyes, above and beyond our understanding. In recent years some have criticized this view, mainly because it seems to give the Father a special degree of divinity, which makes the Son and the Holy Spirit somehow inferior to him. This is always a danger, but as long as we are careful to recognize it and avoid it when it crops up, we can, I think, attribute this to the Father, much in the same way as we attribute the work of redemption to the Son, who alone became incarnate.

Another objection that theologians have raised is that it is wrong to think of God as a "substance" when he is in fact a community of persons. For many people, the word "substance" conjures up an abstract or materialist scientific theory, and one moreover that is no longer current in the scientific world. This may be true, but we do not have to argue over whether God is a "substance" or not before we recognize the Father as the person who manifests the objective being of God in himself, and who in some way gives order and direction to the Trinity as a whole. It is clear from the New Testament that it is the Father who sent the

Son into the world to do his will by saving his people from their sins. We can thus equate him with the God of the Old Testament, because it was precisely this saving will and purpose that God revealed to ancient Israel and that was the ultimate aim of the Mosaic law. Furthermore, if we fail to make this equation, we run the risk of saying that the divine "substance," or whatever we wish to call his being, is a fourth thing, in addition to the three persons of the Trinity. On more than one occasion in the past, scholars have made that accusation; although we seldom hear it today thanks to the tendency to dismiss the concept of "substance" altogether, we cannot be sure that it will not return to the discussion at some future time. If that should happen, we have to be ready to say that the particular work of the Father is to be God simply as God is, remembering that however meaningful our experience of divine immanence may be, we can never contain the transcendent mystery of deity within the limited horizons of our own hearts.

The Inner Life of God: The Person of the Son

Once the person and work of the Father are clear in our minds, we can move back to consider the person of the Son and the theological meaning of "sonship." There is a logic in this, because the Son's work stands in dependence on that of the Father and can only be understood in that light. With respect to the Son's being, what that means in relation to the being of the Father is more complex. Yet the names for the two persons as given to us in Scripture suggest that, however we look at this, the Son stands in second place. At the same time, the Son represents something in the inner life of God that is also true of us, in that we too are called to be sons and in some respect share in his "sonship." The cry of "Abba," the Aramaic word for "father," which the Holy Spirit puts in our hearts, is the cry of the Son; by means of adoption God has admitted us into the Son's relationship with the Father. So characteristic was this of Jesus's teaching that "Abba" became his particular hallmark. When the apostle Paul picks it up and tells his readers that the Spirit of the Son has come into their hearts in order to allow them also to cry "Abba," he is telling them that in the Spirit they have the privilege of being able to speak to the Father in the same way (and therefore with the same authority and assurance) as Jesus did. God has directly patterned our relationship with the Father on that of the Son, so much so that we can almost claim our relationship as assimilated to the Son's relationship within the Godhead.

First of all, let us consider the Son as he stands in relation to the Father. Nowadays, any suggestion of hierarchy or subordination is liable to elicit a strong reaction from those who scent a whiff of Arianism in the air. Others fear that any compromise on the principle of divine equality among the persons of the Godhead may lead to a denial of equality in human relationships, which they see as being modeled on the inner life of God. In answer to these people, we can say that Father and Son imply each other's existence: the names would otherwise be meaningless. You cannot have one without the other. If there were no Son, the First Person of the Trinity would not be the Father; he would have to have some other name that does not imply a parenting relationship. But we must also point out an inner logic in the Father-Son relationship that makes it appropriate for the Son to do the will of the Father, rather than the other way round. Why it should be like this is a mystery, but one thing we do know is that the submission of the Son is voluntary. That is why we must prefer the word "submission" instead of "subordination" or "subjection," both of which imply some form of coercion. Philippians 2:5–11 makes this clear: the apostle Paul tells us that the Son humbled himself and took on the role of a servant, in order to accomplish the work of our salvation. Only someone secure in his relationship of equality with the Father would do this voluntarily. Hence, by what may appear to some as a paradox, it is precisely in the Son's abasement that his true glory as the Father's equal is revealed.

Nevertheless, the sonship that we as believers enjoy in God is not identical to that which belongs to Jesus, although there are significant parallels with it. The essential difference is that whereas Christ by nature is the Son, since the Father has begotten him in eternity, we are sons by adoption. What we cannot claim by virtue of our created being, God has given us by grace, so that we too can become "partakers of the divine nature" (2 Pet. 1:4 KJV). This somewhat curious phrase means that God gives us access to the power of God, which we see at work in our lives.

As God's sons by adoption, we are gradually (but continually) being transformed into the likeness of God's Son by nature, who remains our model and our goal. But the natural Son of God is not some remote divine being, whom we strive in vain to imitate. On the contrary, he became a man in Jesus of Nazareth and lived the life of a normal man. This incarnation was not an end in itself, but a preparation for the supreme act of God in saving us from our sins. Jesus Christ did not just identify himself with us in our humanity; he also became sin for us (2 Cor. 5:21), and took our place at the judgment seat of God. By dying for us in his human nature—our nature—the only-begotten Son of God paid the price for our sins, to deliver us from a burden too great for us to bear on our own. If we do not understand this, we do not understand the gospel, and if we have not died with him in this way, there is no entry for us into the inner life of God.

People have often criticized this belief, which in theological terms is called "penal substitutionary atonement." They do so from thinking that it is somehow immoral of God the Father to send his innocent Son to die for the sins of the human race; but such people have failed to grasp the voluntary nature of the Son's substitution. God the Father never decided to punish his Son on our behalf, and given their fundamental equality within the Godhead, he probably could not have done so even if he had wanted to. It was only when the Son humbled himself and became a servant, to accomplish the Father's will, that the Son became a man, since only in the mode of humanity could he pay the price of our redemption. If there is any "injustice" in this, it is not in the Son's voluntary act on our behalf, but in the fact that we have been redeemed: we have received something from God that we have done nothing to deserve, and that all our own thoughts and desires make us unworthy to obtain.

At the heart of the atonement lies the relationship between the Son and the Father within the Godhead, without which his saving act could not have occurred. We can see this relationship, first of all, in the words that Jesus uttered on the cross, three of which he addressed directly to the Father: "My God, my God, why have you forsaken me?" (Matt. 27:46; Mark 15:34). "Father, forgive them; for they do not know what they are doing" (Luke 23:34). "Father, into your hands I commend my spirit" (Luke 23:46). But we can find echoes of this right through the Gospels, not least in

John, where Jesus is repeatedly explaining his mission in terms of the Father's will, which he has come to accomplish on earth. The roles of the Father and of the Son may be distinguishable, but we can never separate them, since in the end, the divine work of redemption belongs equally to them both. Yet our experience of that redemption does not come directly from either the Father or the Son. Instead, the apostle Paul tells us that God has sent his Son's Spirit into our hearts, making him, a Third Person, the vehicle through whom we enter into God's inner life. Who or what is this Spirit, and why should this be necessary?

The Inner Life of God: The Person of the Holy Spirit

It is no exaggeration to say that in the history of trinitarian theology, the way in which different Christians understand the person and work of the Holy Spirit has caused the most controversy. Even more basic than that, it is hard to know what to make of the many occurrences of the word "spirit" in the New Testament, since it is far from clear just how many of them refer to the Third Person of the Trinity. To go no further than Galatians 4:6, it is not immediately clear from the text that the Spirit of the Son is a distinct person at all. If we knew no more than this, it would be perfectly possible to interpret the phrase simply as a rhetorical device for referring to the Son himself. There are certainly plenty of precedents for this in the Old Testament, which can easily use a phrase like "the Spirit/spirit of God" in this way, and the word "spirit" is sufficiently flexible for it to mean no more than "attitude." For example, what did Jesus mean when he told the Samaritan woman that "God is spirit," and we must worship him in "spirit and truth" (John 4:24)? In the first use of the word "spirit," it seems probable that it refers to God's nonmaterial nature, but the second occurrence is more puzzling. Does it mean that we should worship God in the power of the Holy Spirit, which seems unlikely in the context, or is the word merely referring to the attitude we should adopt in prayer? Most exegetes think that the latter is more probable, and if so, it warns us not to read too much into occurrences of the word "spirit" elsewhere in Scripture if the context does not make a reference to the Third Person of the Trinity inescapable.

Compared with the Father and the Son, the Third Person of the Trinity suffers from being in effect anonymous, since we can apply the words "holy" and "spirit" to many different beings, including righteous people who have died and gone to heaven. His personhood has therefore often been in doubt, and even when it is accepted, his precise relationship to the Father and the Son has long been an area of controversy between Eastern and Western Christians and remains so to this day. The work of the Holy Spirit may be somewhat clearer, at least in outline, but the means by which he effects it have provided endless fodder for debate within the Western church, and have contributed, more than is often realized, to the great divisions between Roman Catholics and Protestants on the one hand, and among different Protestant groups on the other. Indeed, it is probably not too much to say that virtually all the great points of argument between the different denominations of Western Christendom today in the end come down to different ways of understanding the work of the Holy Spirit, both in the church and in individual believers. Why has this complication arisen in Christian theology and brought so much grief in its wake? Do we need a Third Divine Person whose identity is obscure, or can we not make do with the two who so obviously complement one another?

To answer these questions adequately, we have to look at the broader sweep of the New Testament, and in particular at John 14–16, where Jesus explains to his disciples what their experience of God will be like after he has left them. Jesus tells them that he has to go away, because otherwise they will not be able to enter into the fullness of the experience that God has promised them. It is hard to imagine why he tells them that there is something more and indeed better for them than what he has already brought, but that is what he says. After his departure, he will send another Comforter, who will lead them into all truth, enable them to do even greater things than what Jesus has done, and dwell with them forever. What is more, when the other Comforter comes, both Jesus and the Father will come with him, and dwell along with him in their hearts.

From this description of his future activities, it is not difficult to see that the "other Comforter" of John's Gospel is the same Holy Spirit whom Paul mentions in Galatians 4:6 as being the Spirit of the Son, sent by the Father. The Fourth Gospel specifically defines him as proceeding from the Father (John 15:26) and as possessing all the power and authority of Christ himself. Paul's statement is much briefer, but it ties in with John's exposition remarkably well. In Paul's understanding, the Spirit of the Son has the power to enable us to pray as the Son did. For this to be possible, the Spirit must have a relationship to the Father that is equal to that of the Son. If that is the case, then the Holy Spirit must be just as much a person as the Son is, since if he were not, any relationship with the Father that he might have would be fundamentally different from (and necessarily inferior to) that which the Son enjoys. To put this a different way, it is the work of the Holy Spirit in our hearts that makes us confess that he is also a person of the Godhead, and indeed the person through whom we come to understand and experience the other two. Once again, we see that it is the Christian experience of God that obliges Christians to develop a trinitarian confession, since any narrower expression of the relationship between Christian believers and God would be inadequate to explain it.

No one can presume to say why God should have revealed himself to Christians in this way. Yet from what Jesus told his disciples in John 14–16, it is clear that if the Father had not sent the Holy Spirit into our hearts, we would now have an inferior knowledge of God. The Gospels show that the disciples of Jesus had a lesser experience of him before Pentecost than they were to have later, even though they were privileged to see the incarnate Son face to face. As in the Old Testament, God incarnate in Jesus Christ dwelled among his people, but not inside them. They could behold his glory (John 1:14), but in some sense it remained alien to their understanding. Neither his teaching nor his miracles were enough to bridge this gap; at the end of his earthly life, his disciples deserted him because they believed that his mission had been a failure. Jesus had predicted his resurrection, but when it came it was still a surprise to the disciples, who did not quite know what to make of it. In some fundamental way, Jesus remained external to them, and they would not really understand what was going on until they internalized their experience of him and his message. That happened when the Holy Spirit descended on them at Pentecost. Since then, his indwelling presence has been the common possession of the church.

Conclusion

There is much more that one could say about the doctrine
of the Trinity, both as the New Testament reveals it and as the
church has elaborated it on the basis of the biblical data, but the
purpose of this essay has been more limited than that. What I
have demonstrated is that from the earliest recorded evidence
of Christian faith, belief in a Trinity of divine persons has been
an integral part of it. That belief was different from anything
found in Judaism—so different, in fact, that Judaism could not
accommodate it, and Christianity emerged as a new and distinct
religion of its own. Finally, and perhaps most important of all,
I have showed that the Christian doctrine of the Trinity did not
emerge from some kind of philosophical speculation about God,
but from the realities of the Christian spiritual experience of
him. From the beginning, that experience was definitive for the
new faith, and so it has remained ever since. To confess God
as a Trinity is to worship him in our hearts, as those hearts are
stirred by the Spirit of the Son, crying, "Abba! Father!"

3

Faith and Christian Life in the African-American Spirituals

James Earl Massey

The topic of my essay informs you that I have chosen to treat our theme from the standpoint of the faith witness voiced in the religious folk songs, or "spirituals," of African Americans. Behind this choice lie three reasons. First, these historic, history-laden songs, particularly those from the pre-Civil War period, that infamous slavery era, reflect the earliest documented worldview of African-American spirituality. Second, the present hymnological tradition within most branches of the Black church is based upon and echoes the faith perspectives and worldview to which the spirituals give such poignant witness.[1] Third, I have chosen to call attention to these songs because scholars usually overlook their confessional content when they are advancing the interests of theological reflection.

While preparing for this angle of approach, I remembered the experience Howard Thurman had in connection with preparing the Ingersoll Lecture on Immortality he delivered at Harvard Divinity School in 1947. During one of Thurman's annual visits

to Harvard as guest speaker, Willard L. Sperry, Divinity School
dean, invited him to be the Ingersoll Lecturer for 1947. Feeling
honored by the invitation, and well aware that invitations to
give endowed lectures were, at that time, a rarity for Negroes,
Howard Thurman accepted the invitation. When he later wrote
to tell Dean Sperry that he would be discussing immortality
from the faith perspective of the spirituals, Thurman took time
to explain why. As a black scholar he was sensitive to the notion,
quite pervasive at that time, that black scholars were so absorbed
in the struggle for survival in American society that they were
incapable of reflecting creatively on any other matters. Given the
provenance and spiritual pertinence of the spirituals, Thurman
forthrightly explained that he had chosen to treat immortality
from the standpoint of the spirituals in spite of that sometimes
inhibiting notion, and not because of it.[2]

I too have chosen these historic creations because of their
value for treating our theme. I am deeply aware that beyond
what black philosopher Alain Locke referred to as the "ingenu-
ous simplicity"[3] of the spirituals there lie not only social pro-
tests and aspirations but also some instructive and inspiring
theological beliefs and perspectives. There is far more in the
spirituals than poignant poetry and plaintive music; there is also
Scripture-informed, soul-engaging, prophetic musings about
God, human life, Christian faith, spirituality, personal responsibility, and human destiny.

Spirituals

In referring to these songs as "spirituals," I honor a respected
tradition. While they are by category religious folk songs, they
are by content and intent "spirituals," although writers have used
and can use several other descriptions for them. Influenced by
the heart-wrenching history that inspired these songs, W. E. B.
DuBois called them "sorrow songs."[4] Mindful of the settings in
which they were fashioned and used, during and after slavery,
Booker T. Washington referred to these songs as "plantation
melodies."[5] After researching the history of these creations and
the strivings and aspirations they voice, historian Miles Mark
Fisher discussed them as "Negro Slave Songs."[6] Impressed by

the number of these songs, their folk origins, topical range, and transforming applications, musicologist John Lovell Jr. honored those who fashioned these songs when he referred to these creations collectively as "Black Song."[7] As for the universal importance of "song" itself in human life, Scotsman Thomas Carlyle in one of his writings alertly suggested that music is our deepest human reality: "All inmost things . . . naturally utter themselves in Song." "All deep things are Song. It seems somehow the very central essence of us, Song; as if all the rest were but wrappages and hulls." "See deep enough," Carlyle continued, "and you see musically."[8]

The deep substructure of the spirituals, the foundation on which they rest and from which they rise, is faith. These songs reflect and promote black beliefs, hopes, and aspirations rooted in faith: faith in the creative, all-powerful, delivering, sustaining, energizing, and fulfilling activity of a just and loving God. This faith content gave strength to their intentions for use: to inform, encourage, sustain, and inspire. Thus, Howard Thurman makes a convictional comment: "The clue to the meaning of the spirituals is to be found in religious experience and spiritual discernment."[9] A response of dynamic African sensibilities to teachings drawn from both Testaments of Scripture, insights from the processes of nature, and raw experiences in life—the spirituals are songs of faith content sung and used with intent. They were originally expressive instrumental agencies to give witness, to teach, to nurture, to remind, to encourage, to sustain, to convict, to convince, to inspire.

God in the Spirituals

In 1938, Benjamin Elijah Mays published an important study entitled *The Negro's God*. The purpose of that study was, in his words, "to tell America what the Negro thinks of God."[10] That book was a first of its kind. It was based on Negro literature dating from as early as 1760, and the researched corpus included slave narratives, biography, autobiography, addresses, novels, poetry, prayers, sermons, catechetical productions for church use, and spirituals. While the entire book is informative, it is particularly valuable as the first attempt by any scholar to study the development of the idea of God in the literature of African Americans. I call attention to what Mays discovered and reported about ideas of God as expressed in 122 spirituals he examined:

> The ideas reflected in the Spirituals may be briefly summarized: God is omnipotent, omnipresent, and omniscient. In both Heaven and earth God is sovereign. He is a just God. . . . God is revengeful. . . . God is a warrior and He fights the battles of His chosen people. . . . God takes care of His own. He will see to it that the righteous are vindicated and that the heavily laden are given rest from the troubles of the world. . . . God is near and there is a feeling of dependence upon Him. In times of distress, He is ever present. . . . He answers prayers. . . . God is observant. He sees all you do and He hears all you say.[11]

There is more in that book, far more, but I have mentioned enough to show that these ideas in the spirituals regarding God are traditionally biblical. The spirituals appropriated some ideas directly from the Bible, such as God being a warrior and deliverer, as illustrated in "Go Down, Moses" and "Joshua Fit de Battle ob Jericho." Statements and accounts reported in the Bible stimulated other ideas, such as God being always near and observant. In any instance, these God ideas in the spirituals are in agreement with what the Bible expresses about God.

The spirituals devote special attention to God as deliverer. Some of the most vibrant lines treat God's dramatic work in changing situations for certain biblical characters, or using chosen characters to change situations for others, as in this reference:

> "Thus spoke the Lord," bold Moses said;
>   "Let my people go,
> If not I'll smite your firstborn dead,
>   Let my people go."[12]

Or this reference to Joshua in the well-known song that honors him:

> You may talk about yo' king ob Gideon,
> You may talk about yo' man ob Saul,
> Dere's none like good ole Joshua,
> At de battle ob Jericho.[13]

In connection with this Joshua song and its message of a sovereign God who acts to deliver the oppressed, John Lovell Jr. has commented: "Only the most naive reader [or singer or listener] misses the point that what Joshua did can be done again and again, wherever wrong and evil are to be overthrown, wherever promised good and right are to be established."[14] The same message comes through in the spiritual "Didn't My Lord Deliver Daniel?"

> He delivered Daniel f'om de lion's den,
>   Jonah f'om de belly of de whale,
> An' de Hebrew chillun f'om de fiery furnace,
>   An' why not every man?[15]

The dominant view expressed in the spirituals about God is of a sovereign Creator who has the whole of life under his care, and that, being God, he will make things right in the end:

> God is a God!
> God don't never change!
> God is a God
> An' He always will be God!
> The earth His footstool
> an' heav'n His throne,
> The whole creation all His own,
> His love an' power will prevail,
> His promises will never fail.
> God is a God!
> An' always will be God![16]

Jesus in the Spirituals

The most important thing one can say about the representation of Jesus in the spirituals is that they never view him as a distant figure, or only an object of faith, but always as a living person whose warmth, concern, love, trustworthiness, helpfulness, power, steadiness, example, and availability we can experience. The spirituals understand that Jesus is Son of God and Christ. Although these titles basically describe his personhood, they do not adequately convey his personality as the singers experience and regard him. By "personality" I refer to the personal attributes and traits that allow us to anticipate and value his behavior toward those who in openness and faith approach him.

The spirituals evidence a relationship with Jesus, a valued familiarity and companionship with him as religious subject. Jesus is one who knows life as the singers knew it, and one who knows them as suffering suppliants as well.

We can readily trace the impact of the circumstances and plight of the Hebrews upon those who created and sang the spirituals. Knowledge of that nation's deliverance by God from struggles helped the singers to discern the nature of God and to trust God's power. But while Old Testament narratives provided dramatic resources for faith, the New Testament story about Jesus sensitized the slave singers, especially accounts of his arrest, trial, and crucifixion. Jesus's approach to his experiences informed them for facing and handling their experiences. They identified with Jesus, deeply aware that he had already identified himself with them:

> Dey crucified my Lord,
> An' he never said a mumbalin' word.
> Dey crucified my Lord,
> An' he never said a mumbalin' word.
> Not a word—not a word—not a word.[17]

Among the many other oft-sung elegies about our Lord's ordeal as suffering Savior, there is that unique and universally beloved spiritual that asks, "Were You There When They Crucified My Lord?"[18] In that spiritual, the singers confessed their understanding and voiced their lament concerning that processed event Jesus underwent: they speak of Jesus being "nailed to the tree," "pierced in the side," and "laid in the tomb," and they responded to the meaning of it all with full openness of soul:

> Were you there when they crucified my Lord?
> Were you there when they crucified my Lord?
> Oh, sometimes it causes me to tremble, tremble, tremble.
> Were you there when they crucified my Lord?

In his autobiography Howard Thurman tells about the visit he and his wife, Sue, had with Mahatma Gandhi while in India in 1935 as guests of the Student Christian Movement of India, Burma, and Ceylon. After a long visit with deep conversations, as their allotted time with the Mahatma came to a close, Gandhi asked the Thurmans not to leave before favoring him by singing one of the Negro spirituals. He specifically requested that they sing "Were You There When They Crucified My Lord?" with the comment, "I feel that this song gets to the root of the experience of the entire human race under the spread of the healing wings of suffering." Mrs. Thurman, an Oberlin Conservatory of Music graduate, led in singing that spiritual as Gandhi and his associates bowed their heads in prayer.[19] Although Gandhi sensed something of universal import in the undeserved suffering Jesus underwent, we lament that he missed the expiatory meaning of Jesus's death. The slave singers did not miss that meaning. They understood his death as an atoning deed, and they rejoiced about it as a completed task:

> Hallelujah t' de Lamb,
> Jesus died for every man.
> But He ain't comin' here t' die no mo',
> Ain't comin' here t' die no mo.
>
> He died for de blind, He died for de lame,
> He bore de pain an' all de blame.
> But He ain't comin' here t' die no mo',
> Ain't comin' here t' die no mo.[20]

Several spirituals treat the Lord's resurrection, but representative of the note of victory sounded in them all is the spiritual "Dust an' Ashes," also known as "An' de Lord Shall Bear My Spirit Home."[21] First the spiritual acknowledges that death does its work on all humans: "Dust, dust an' ashes fly over on my grave." It goes on to voice faith that death is not the end: "An' de Lord shall bear my spirit home." Successive stanzas picture the Lord's crucifixion, the burial of his body in Joseph's tomb, the descent of an angel to roll the stone from the entrance, and then—death's loss:

> De cold grave could not hold Him,
> Nor death's cold iron band,
> An' de Lord shall bear my spirit home,
> An' de Lord shall bear my spirit home.

> He rose, He rose, He rose from de dead.
> He rose, He rose, He rose from de dead,
> He rose, He rose, He rose from de dead,
> An' de Lord shall bear my spirit home.

The point of witness is clear: what God did for Jesus, God is going to do for those who believe on Jesus.

Regarding the Christian life, the creators of spirituals were deeply concerned about the inner life of the soul. They sensed, quite rightly, that sincere religion and courageous living call for a heart that God has touched and controls. Being enslaved, oppressed, and unfairly treated, there were times when the heart's attitudes provoked alarm and dismay, times when the impulse to deal with things on a purely selfish basis was strong, so a penitent appeal was made to God or Jesus for help:

> 'Tis me, 'tis me, 'tis me, O Lord,
> Standin' in the need of prayer.
> 'Tis me, 'tis me, 'tis me, O Lord,
> An' I'm standin' in the need of prayer.[22]

The singers knew that God and Jesus give aid for character change. That was the concern behind these lines:

> Lord, I want to be a Christian
> In-a my heart, in-a-my heart,
> Lord, I want to be more loving
> In-a my heart.
> I don't want to be like Judas
> In-a my heart.
> Lord, I want to be like Jesus
> In-a my heart.[23]

The insistence was always upon faith in Jesus, trust in him as a concerned helper, an understanding companion, a brother, although he is also Lord.

> Oh, Jesus my Saviour,
> On Thee I'll depend,
> When troubles are near me,
> You'll be my true friend.[24]

Given the peace and hope from an experienced relation with Jesus, the spirituals did not even view dying as an ultimate threat:

> You needn't mind my dying,
> You needn't mind my dying,
> You needn't mind my dying,
> Jesus goin' to make up my dying bed.[25]

This attitude of confidence in God and sense of companionship with Jesus, including even in the hour of death, is never absent from the spirituals. Urgency of need and sincere longing of soul made these seekers strive for survival, courage, solace, stability, and meaning. To gain these benefits the sufferers had to reach for the ultimate. In seeking the ultimate, informed by biblical truths, they found the Triune God. Thus comes the Christian orthodoxy these songs reflect.

The Holy Spirit in the Spirituals

The biblical teachings about the Holy Spirit point beyond themselves in two directions: one direction is Godward, disclosing that in the Godhead a Third Person is related to God the Father and Jesus the Son; the other direction is humanward, declaring that God relates to his open and obedient children in intimate and inward ways.

According to Romans 8:1–17 and Galatians 5:16–25, among other passages of instruction, the Christian life is lived "in" and "by" the Spirit. The spirituals usually assume the pervasive presence of the Holy Spirit with the believer, but they rarely make direct references to the Spirit. There are spirituals showing experience of the deep intimacy between God and the soul as a sense of divine possession that makes one feel settled and secure, settled in grace and secure in God's love. Voiced affirmations by African-American Christians about divine grace and a sense of being filled or possessed by the Spirit are still two of the most persistent features in African-American worship. Regarding God's grace, Henry H. Mitchell has explained: "No mere theological nicety, the grace of God was and is to the Black [person] a means of life and strength—a source of support and balance and self-certainty in a world whose approval of Blacks is still in extremely short supply."[26] We can understand being filled or possessed by the Spirit as an experience of feeling settled, energized, and emboldened by the Holy Spirit. This is surely reflected in the spiritual "Dere's a Little Wheel a-Turnin' in My Heart":

> O, I don't feel no ways tired in my heart,
> In my heart, in my heart,
> O, I don't feel no ways tired in my heart.
>
> I've a double 'termination in my heart,
> In my heart, in my heart,
> I've a double 'termination in my heart.[27]

After the heart has surrendered to God's claiming grace, God has witnessed his approval through his Spirit. The Spirit grants a convictional knowledge to the believer that God has become intimately linked with oneself, as in lines like these:

> O, I know the Lord,
> I know the Lord,
> I know the Lord's laid His hands on me.[28]

Such songs witness about a life activated and controlled from a new and ultimate center.

In one of those rare instances where the lyric directly mentions the Holy Spirit, that particular spiritual understands him as one who "moves" or motivates the believer to prayer. Perhaps Romans 8:26 and/or Ephesians 6:18 influenced this view:

> Ev'ry time I feel the Spirit,
> move-in' in my heart,
> I will pray.
> O, ev'ry time I feel the Spirit,
> move-in' in my heart,
> I will pray.[29]

The simple assumption regarding the Holy Spirit is that he joins the believer's life in a sensed filling and "possession," granting an awareness of belonging (Rom. 8:16) and of being girded (Luke 24:49). I use that expression "sensed possession" purposely but advisedly. Though it would be a mistake to identify the inward witness of the Spirit solely with what one can feel and physically express in shout or movement, it is likewise a mistake to overlook the fact that feeling—the deepest, most immediate, and most vivid human experience—is sometimes the means by which the Holy Spirit allows us to realize his inward ministry to us. The singers understood this, and while some of them certainly enjoyed and expected times of "holy overwhelming" in their religious experience, they also sang about those private times when the Holy Spirit brought needed encouragement and renewal to their life:

> Sometimes I feel discouraged,
> And think my work's in vain,
> But then the Holy Spirit
> Revives my soul again.[30]

The human condition involves us in a range of experiences demanding that the Christian have a focused selfhood. One achieves that focus with the help of the possessing and renewing presence of the Holy Spirit within us. Our becoming, our growth in grace, is dependent upon the goals and means exhibited in Jesus and mediated within us by the Holy Spirit. The believer, helped by the Holy Spirit, receives strengthened resolve and readiness to live for God and to face any conflicts and opposition:

> Done made my vow to the Lord
> and I never will turn back,
> I will go, I shall go, to see what the end will be.
> Done opened my mouth to the Lord
> and I never will turn back,
> I will go, I shall go, to see what the end will be.[31]

The singers understood that the steadiness and stamina needed to fulfill such a vow depends upon a believer being possessed and enabled by the Holy Spirit.

Conclusion

I have been reviewing the Christian witness in some of the historic spirituals, those worded songs about God, Jesus, the Holy

Spirit, and Christian life. Biblical truths and imagery influenced these songs, and African-American sensibilities and social experience shaped them. These spirituals, with many others, reflect faith. They bear witness, reinforce meanings, inspire worship, and sustain hope. They give us poignant music and so much more. They give us prophetic musings, flavored by the history, longings, experiences, religious discoveries, and faith of a life-tested people. These songs nurture self-respect. They echo a biblical theology. They voice an affirmative theodicy. They mirror the African-American soul. They helped, and still help, a seeking people to face dark times and meet the exigencies of life with faith, fortitude, and essential pride. These songs are an important repository of spiritual insight, and duly regarded, they stir one to faithfulness, praise, and practical theological reflection.

4

The Trinity and Christian Unity

Avery Cardinal Dulles, S.J.

The Trinity as Principle of Unity

At the beginning of the Christian life stands baptism, the rite consecrating the individual to God—the Father, the Son, and the Holy Spirit. Baptism, accompanied by a profession of faith, is administered in many different churches and ecclesial communities and thus forges uniting bonds of deep ecumenical significance. Every Christian is marked by special relationships with the Father, the Son, and the Holy Spirit.

Christian initiation brings us, first of all, into a personal family relationship with God the Father, the creator of heaven and earth, who instituted the saving plan to redeem the world through his Son. We receive the courage to call upon him as our Father and to see ourselves as his sons and daughters.

When believers call upon God as their Father, they manifest a family bond that transcends all ecclesiastical divisions. In what we might today call an ecumenical spirit, Augustine pleads eloquently with his flock to recognize baptism as a bond of union between them and the Donatists:

> We entreat you, brothers, as earnestly as we are able, to have charity, not only for one another, but also for those who are outside the Church. Of these some are still pagans, who have not yet made an act of faith in Christ. Others are separated, insofar as they are joined with us in professing faith in Christ, our head, but are yet divided from the unity of his body. My friends, we must grieve over our brothers. Whether they like it or not, they are our brothers; and they will only cease to be so when they no longer say "our Father". . . .
>
> Those who tell us: "You are not our brothers," are saying that we are pagans. That is why they want to baptize us again, claiming that we do not have what they can give. Hence their error in denying that we are their brothers. Why then did the prophet tell us: "Say to them: You are our brothers"? It is because we acknowledge in them that which we do not repeat. By not recognizing our baptism, they deny that we are their brothers; on the other hand, when we do not repeat their baptism but acknowledge it to be our own, we are saying to them, "You are our brothers."
>
> If they say, "Why do you seek us? What do you want of us?" we should reply, "You are our brothers." They may say, "Leave us alone. We have nothing to do with you." But we have everything to do with you, for we are one in our belief in Christ; and so we should be in our body, under one head.[1]

It would be a great ecumenical advance if we who are here today could agree that as long as we all look to God as our Father in Christ, we remain brothers and sisters.

Augustine, in the passage just quoted, dwells primarily on the relationship between baptized Christians and God the Father. But that relationship is inseparable from affinity with the incarnate Son, Jesus Christ, the revealer of the Father. In the New Testament, Paul calls Jesus "the firstborn among many brothers," thanks to whom we are adopted sons and daughters of the Father (Rom. 8:29 NIV).

In the sense here used by Paul, adoption is much more than a legal fiction. By baptism we are immersed in the death of Jesus and are raised again to newness of life. Paul can therefore write to the Colossians: "When you were buried with him in baptism, you were also raised with him through faith in the power of God, who raised him from the dead" (Col. 2:12; cf. Rom. 6:3–4).

We should not overlook the social and ecclesial implications of Christian initiation. In several of his letters Paul makes it clear that all the baptized are incorporated into Christ and thus are made members of his body. To the Galatians he writes: "As many of you as were baptized into Christ have clothed yourselves with Christ. . . . For all of you are one in Christ Jesus" (Gal. 3:27–28). In the mystical view of Paul, Christians live in Christ and Christ lives in them. For Paul, as we know, the church is the body of Christ, an extension of his individual, physical body. If baptism is the rite of incorporation, we must conclude that all baptized believers are one in the body of Christ, which is the church. Vatican II's Decree on Ecumenism acknowledges this: "All those justified by faith through baptism are incorporated into Christ. They therefore have a right to be honored by the title of Christian, and are properly regarded as brothers and sisters in the Lord by the children of the Catholic Church" (Unitatis redintegratio [UR] 3; cf. 22). Because we think of the church comprehensively as the body of Christ, our ecclesiology ought to be broadly ecumenical. This christological perspective will bring us far beyond a merely sociological view that would restrict church membership to the rolls of any denomination or group of denominations.

Through faith and baptism, Christians enter into relations not only with the Father and the Son, but also with the Third Divine Person. Believers in the lordship of Jesus, even though they belong to different ecclesial communities, are sharers in the one Holy Spirit, for as Paul teaches, "No one can say 'Jesus is Lord' except by the Holy Spirit" (1 Cor. 12:3). In the Spirit we have access not only to the Son but also to the Father (Eph. 2:18). Thanks to the Spirit who dwells within us, we are able to recognize that we are sons and daughters and to cry out "Abba! Father!" (Rom. 8:15; cf. Gal. 4:5). The New Testament variously attributes divine indwelling to the Father, the Son, and the Holy Spirit. At the Last Supper Jesus promises that he and the Father, together with the Holy Spirit, will come to dwell lovingly in those who love him and keep his commandments (John 14:16–17, 23). Paul speaks of Christ dwelling in our hearts through faith (Eph.

3:17). But in the same context he teaches that we are made into dwelling places of God by the Holy Spirit (Eph. 2:22). The Second Letter to Timothy speaks of the Holy Spirit who dwells within us (1:14). In a number of texts Paul declares that individual Christians—and indeed the church as a whole (Eph. 2:21)—are temples of the Holy Spirit (1 Cor. 3:16; 6:19). Taking these and similar texts in unison, it seems fair to conclude that through the gift of the Holy Spirit, all three divine persons dwell intimately within those justified by grace.

We frequently speak of the charisms or gifts bestowed by the Holy Spirit, but we often fail to notice that in the classic biblical text on the subject, Paul states that we should see the gifts of the Spirit as the operations of the Father and as administrations of the Lord (1 Cor. 12:4–26). Under different aspects, therefore, believers can attribute the gifts to the Father, the Son, and the Holy Spirit. The outwardly directed actions of the Triune God are from all three persons, who work together. As Augustine memorably said, "The Holy Spirit does not dwell in anyone without the Father and the Son, just as the Son does not without the Father and the Holy Spirit, nor does the Father without them. They are inseparable in their dwelling, just as they are in their working, but they are usually indicated by one through created symbols, not in their own substance." Indwelling, he goes on to say, is appropriated to the Holy Spirit, who is somehow "the companionship of the Father and the Son."[2] He is the bond of peace and unity (Rom. 8:6; 14:17; Gal. 5:22). Paul speaks of *koinōnia*, which is translated as either "communion" or "fellowship." In the blessing at the end of 2 Corinthians, he writes: "The grace of our Lord Jesus Christ, the love of God, and the . . . [*koinōnia*] of the Holy Spirit be with all of you" (13:13–14).

The preceding considerations regarding baptized believers and the three divine persons have immense implications for the ecumenical task. They tell us that Christians, notwithstanding their ecclesiastical divisions, already have a significant measure of communion or fellowship. The doctrine of the Trinity, while it is not the totality of our beliefs, is absolutely fundamental to all our churches. Beyond this, belief in the Trinity shows the way to deepening the communion we already have. The more closely each of us is conjoined to the Father, the Son, and the Holy Spirit, the closer shall we be to one another. If in some measure we are alienated from one another, it is because some or all of us are insufficiently united to the Triune God.

Body of Christ and Interpersonal Communion

These trinitarian texts are of crucial importance not only for our personal spirituality but also for our sense of the church. Since the high Middle Ages, at least in the West, ecclesiology, both Protestant and Catholic, has tended to be almost exclusively Christocentric. It has suffered from what Yves Congar and others call Christomonism. In the Catholic tradition, Vatican II sounded a call to go beyond this constriction and to develop a richly trinitarian ecclesiology, more harmonious with the Eastern Orthodox tradition. Far from being an innovation, such an ecclesiology would be a return to the ante-Nicene fathers, Western as well as Eastern. Tertullian, for example, wrote in his treatise on baptism: "Wherever the three are (that is, the Father, the Son, and the Holy Spirit), there is the Church, which is the body of the three."[3] While commenting on the Lord's Prayer and its petition for forgiveness, Cyprian describes the church as "a people made one with the unity of the Father, the Son, and the Holy Spirit."[4]

We should not reject the Christocentric ecclesiology so deeply built into the Catholic tradition in favor of a Spirit-centered ecclesiology. The church in all truth is the body of Christ. Organic metaphors such as "body of Christ" and "vine" express an important biblical datum. The church is not just a moral or sociological entity. The bonds between the members are ontological, so that the church and Christ together make up, in a mystical sense, one person: *una persona mystica*, as Thomas Aquinas put it.[5] But these organic metaphors, like all analogies, have their limitations. They do not by themselves bring out the interpersonal structure of the church. Christians are not just parts of a supernatural organism; they are free and intelligent subjects who enter into personal relations with God.

The trinitarian ecclesiology that has become so prominent since Vatican II has arisen in an atmosphere of personalism. Toward the middle of the twentieth century, European philosophers and theologians became newly conscious of the uniqueness and dignity of each individual person. In this intellectual environment it became possible and necessary to point out that the church is not just a thing, even a sacred thing; it is made up of persons in multifaceted relations with other persons. The relationships within the Christian community are especially intimate because they are grounded in a relationship with God, or rather, as we have just seen, with the three divine persons. Theologians are accustomed to designate this relationship by the technical term "communion." To alert the reader to the technical usage, the term is frequently expressed in Greek, *koinōnia*, or in Latin, *communio*, thus distinguishing it from other uses of the term "communion." The church, in this framework, is called a *communio personarum*, an interpersonal communion.

As a prime biblical text authorizing this trinitarian ecclesiology, I choose John 17:21. At the Last Supper, in his final conversation with the apostles as a group, Jesus prays to his Father that his disciples may be one. "As you, Father, are in me and I am in you, may they also be in us, so that the world may believe that you have sent me." In other passages, as we have recognized, Jesus speaks of the indwelling of the divine persons within the individual believer, but in this text he is focusing on the union among believers. It is to be a reflection of, and participation in, the perfect unity among the divine persons—the Father, the Son, and by implication, the Holy Spirit. As Vatican II commented in its Decree on Ecumenism, the "source and exemplar" of the unity of Christians is "the unity, in the Trinity of persons, of the one God, the Father and the Son, in the Holy Spirit" (UR 2). The Decree on the Church's Missionary Activity depicts the church as participating in the mission of the Son from the Father and of the Holy Spirit from the Father through the Son (Ad gentium [AG] 2). Contemporary theologians frequently refer to the church as "icon of the Trinity."[6]

Fellowship in the Trinity, then, makes the church much more than a society of friends, in the ordinary sense of the word. It also is a participation in the communion of the divine persons. And the participation is to be so visible and striking that it will challenge the world to believe. If the world does not believe, the failure of Christians to achieve and manifest the oneness of which Christ speaks is no doubt a major contributing cause. The final prayer of Jesus in the upper room is therefore a key text for ecumenism in the service of Christian mission.

To carry this line of thought further, we must reflect on the kind of unity that obtains among the divine persons. According to the dogmatic decisions of the early church, which are normative for most of our traditions, the union among them is not simply that of an association of like-minded persons. The union is not merely moral but also ontological. The Father and the Son are *homoousioi*. Numerically one in substance or nature, they are distinguished from one another only by their relations of personal origin. For this reason Christians are able to worship three divine persons without falling into polytheism.

The fellowship of Christians cannot exactly replicate that of the divine persons. As human beings, we are distinct substances, and our relationships are, unlike those in the Godhead, accidents. We can acquire or lose these relationships without ceasing to be ourselves. Only in a metaphorical sense can we become, in the terminology of Acts 4:32, one in heart and soul. We are, and shall eternally remain, distinct substances with our own minds and wills. I therefore propose the unity of the divine persons as an ideal for us to approach from afar, the asymptotic goal of our hopes and endeavors.

Reflections of Particular Divine Persons

Contemporary ecclesiologists who adhere to a trinitarian model of the church do not all agree about what kind of unity this model requires. Different theologies of the Trinity call for different ecclesiologies, and conversely, different ecclesiologies lead to different theologies of the Trinity. Some theologians accept a hierarchical model; others, an egalitarian model.

According to the classical theological tradition, especially strong in the Eastern fathers, there is an order among the divine persons. The Father is the fontal source, the one principle, exercising what is called monarchy (*monarchia*). The Son is, as we say in the Nicene Creed, "God from God, . . . true God from true God." For his divinity and personal existence, he is totally dependent on the Father, who communicates to him everything that he, the Son, is and has. The Spirit proceeds from the Father and, according to the Western tradition, from the Son as well. The relations of origin are not reversible. They give rise to an order in missions. The Father cannot be sent. The Son can be sent, but only by the Father (John 8:42). The Holy Spirit is sent by the Father and the Son (John 15:26; Acts 2:33). The Son can do nothing except what the Father tells him to do (John 5:19–20; 8:28); the Holy Spirit cannot say anything except what the Father and Son tell him to say (John 16:13).

If the church is to be an icon of the Trinity, it must reflect the three divine persons. In its mission the church must obey the Father, who sends it. In its structures and offices the church must represent the Son, its founder. And in its life the church must embody the Holy Spirit, who animates it from within.

Can we proceed further and identify different offices or functions in the church with one or other of the divine persons? At this point we drift into deep waters, where the navigation is not easy. Since others have speculated on this question, I shall assess some things others have said.

The Eastern emperors, according to some scholars, thought of themselves as embodying the paternal principle. They reportedly favored Arianism because it supported a strong monarchy in which the whole church was subject to a single ruler, as Arius held the Son and Holy Spirit to be subject to the Father. But in this case, as in others, the effort to manipulate the doctrine for political purposes led to heresy.[7]

In the nineteenth century, Vladimir Soloviev tried to apply trinitarian ecclesiology to the problem of Christian reunion. He identified the Catholic Church with the Father, the Petrine principle, and the kingly office. The Orthodox Church, in his view, reflected the Son, the Johannine principle, and the priestly office. The Protestant churches, for their part, expressed the Holy Spirit, the Pauline principle, and the prophetic office. Soloviev conjectured that the three might come together into a union reflecting that of the Trinity if each tradition would give due recognition to the special prerogatives of the other two. Cardinal Joseph Ratzinger, now Pope Benedict XVI, faults him for suggesting that the doctrine of the Trinity might be able to support the kind of ecclesial diversity represented by Catholicism, Orthodoxy, and Protestantism. Could the primacy, Ratzinger asks, be shared by a Catholic, an Orthodox, and a Reformed Christian composing a kind of divine troika?[8]

Soloviev's musings are not easy to interpret. If he meant to suggest that it would be enough for a church to express the characteristics attributed to some one divine person, his position would be defective. Any properly constituted church must participate in the perfections of all three. The church is necessarily from the Father, who sends it into the world; from the Son, whose mystical body it is; and from the Holy Spirit, without whose animating presence the church could not fulfill its commission from the Father and the Son. The church must therefore be Petrine, Johannine, and Pauline; it must be kingly, priestly, and prophetic.

In recent decades some theologians have been revisiting the doctrine of the Trinity with the hope of promoting a more democratic church order. These authors frequently appeal to the concept of circumincession, or *perichōrēsis*, that has been prominent in Greek theology. Circumincession is certainly a sound doctrine if it is taken to mean the mutual indwelling of the divine persons, a theme that surfaces more than once in the Gospel of John ("The Father is in me and I am in the Father," 10:38; cf. 17:21). But to take the *perichōrēsis* as evidence that the order of processions is mutual or reversible is a misunderstanding. Jürgen Moltmann and Miroslav Volf, for example, depict the trinitarian relations as reciprocal and polycentric.[9] Because of the eternal circulation of the divine life, they hold, the three divine persons are strictly equal; they live and are manifested in one another and through one another.[10] "The cycle of self-donations," writes Volf, "must start moving simultaneously at all points."[11] "Hierarchical constructions of the trinitarian relations," he contends, "appear from this perspective as projections of the fascination with earthly hierarchies onto the heavenly community."[12] This nonhierarchical rendering of trinitarian theology is apparently dictated by a desire to justify a democratic or congregational church order.

Joseph Ratzinger proposes a quite different analogy between the Trinity and ecclesiastical governance. Recent denials of the divine monarchy, he contends, are distortions of the faith under the pressure of church politics. According to the constant witness of Holy Scripture, he asserts, community leadership is not in the first instance collegial; it is inseparable from personal responsibility. The principle of "one responsible person," he writes, is "anchored fast in the Trinitarian belief in God itself, since the Trinity becomes meaningful and in fact recognizable for us through the fact that in his Son as man God himself has become witness to himself." The Son in turn designated Peter as the rock and the bearer of the church's creed. The Petrine ministry "can only exist as a person and in personal responsibility tied to a particular name."[13] In ascribing primacy to the "monarchical" bishop in the local church, and to the successor of Peter for the universal church, Ratzinger is not justifying domination or oppression, but calling for a church ordered in truth and freedom. Just as God the Father rules in order to give life, so on earth the hierarchical ministers have power only for the purpose of service.

Ratzinger's view of monarchical church leadership does not lack support from the patristic tradition. Ignatius of Antioch finds an analogy between the Father's position in the Trinity and that of the monarchical bishop in the local church. To the Magnesians he writes: "Strive to do all things in the harmony that God wills, under the direction of the bishop who holds the place of God, and of the presbyters who stand in place of the apostolic college, and with my dearest deacons, to whom is entrusted the service of Jesus Christ."[14] Ignatius instructs the church of Smyrna: "As Jesus Christ follows the Father, so all of you must follow the bishop and the presbyterate, as if they were the apostles."[15]

The question of primacy in the universal church inevitably came to the fore in the course of time. Ignatius alludes only vaguely to the universal primacy, speaking of the Roman church as the one that presides in charity.[16] A little later Irenaeus contends that the church of Rome, "founded by the two most glorious apostles Peter and Paul," has a higher primacy (*potentiorem principalitatem*) than other apostolic sees, so that every church must agree with it.[17] In the Constantinian era the major apostolic sees were regarded as giving regional primacy to their respective churches—those of Rome, Alexandria, Antioch, Jerusalem, and eventually also Constantinople. But because Peter ranked first among the apostles, the church of Rome was seen as enjoying a universal primacy.

Can the primacy of Rome be grounded in trinitarian theology? Thomas Aquinas believed that it could. In his tract *Against the*

Errors of the Greeks, he wrote rather cryptically that because the Holy Spirit proceeds from the Father and the Son, the Roman pontiff, as vicar of Christ, must have primacy over the universal church.[18] As I understand him, Thomas is here ascribing the concord among the bishops to the influence of the Holy Spirit. If the Spirit does not proceed from the Son, that concord would be independent of the pope, who represents the Son as his vicar. For Thomas it seems evident that the vicar of Christ must have primacy, since the Father gives the incarnate Son headship over the church (Col. 1:18), and the incarnate Son transmits the keys of authority to Peter as head of the apostolic college (Matt. 16:18–19).

According to the tradition, collegiality is appropriated to the Holy Spirit.[19] The consensus of the bishops is a sign and effect of their common sharing in the Spirit. If the Spirit also proceeds from the Son, and not from the Father alone, the pneumatic dimension of the church comes into being through the pope, who visibly represents Christ the head. On the analogy of the divine *perichōrēsis*, one may further illustrate the interlocking between primacy and collegiality in the episcopate. In the words of Bruno Forte:

> Just as there is a relationship to the image of the divine "perichoresis" among the churches, so between the bishop of Rome and the other bishops there exists a true "perichoresis" in the episcopate, which takes nothing away from the primacy [of the pope] nor from the dignity of each of the other bishops, just as, analogously, the "monarchy" of the Father in the Trinity takes nothing away from the dignity and integrity of the other Persons.[20]

Particular Churches in the Universal Church

The bishop, if he is head of a diocese, has two different relationships to the Trinity. As a member of the order or college of bishops, he represents the pneumatic or collegial principle vis-à-vis the pope, his primate. As the governor of a diocese, however, the bishop represents the primatial or monarchical principle, whereas the college of presbyters, as we have heard from Ignatius of Antioch, embodies the pneumatic or collegial principle.

The church was founded as a universal society, open to people of every tribe and tongue. An independent national or regional church would violate the universal unity of the church, which is by nature neither American nor European, neither Southern nor Northern, but all-inclusive. By faith and baptism we enter into this one church. Every particular church is, as Vatican II put it, "fashioned after the model of the universal Church" (Lumen gentium [LG] 23; cf. AG 20).

The ontological priority of the universal church does not contradict the fact that the church initially came into being in a particular locality. Louis Bouyer puts the matter well:

> [Peter] founded the Church on Pentecost by announcing the risen Christ to those around him, by baptizing, by having "those who had believed" baptized by his apostolic coworkers, by having them share in the first celebration of the eucharistic banquet and by thus involving them in a common life of thanksgiving and charity. The Church of all times and all places was founded, then, in the first local Church, that of Jerusalem, and she was propagated from this Church in similar local Churches by planting cuttings, as it were from the shoot.[21]

Initially, the local church of Jerusalem was not a particular church within some larger universal communion; it coincided with the universal church. Particular churches, which were less than universal, arose when the church expanded so that the faithful could no longer assemble in one place under a single set of pastors. The multiplicity of communities does not divide the church because, through a kind of *perichōrēsis*, they are in full communion with one another. They acknowledge one another's pastors and members; the same faith is preached and the same sacraments are administered in all of them.[22]

Guarding against any tendency to reduce diocesan churches to the status of a huge corporation's administrative districts, Vatican II asserted that each particular church is a realization of the universal church in a given locality. The church, it stated, is most palpably realized in the liturgical assembly, when the sacraments are celebrated.[23] Paul had already depicted the Eucharist as the unifying force in the local church. The faithful of Corinth, he wrote, were one body because they received the true body of Christ, truly present in the Eucharist (1 Cor. 10:17). The offering of the Eucharist under the presidency of the residential bishop and his assistant clergy, with the full participation of the faithful, is a palmary realization of the church. The Eucharist is the sacrament of unity not only for the local but also for the universal church.

With the help of this *koinōnia* theology, Vatican II sought to rehabilitate not only the local (or diocesan) church but also regional churches, assimilating these in certain respects with the ancient patriarchates. The unity of the church includes a certain pluriformity, since it allows for groups of churches that "organically united, . . . enjoy their own discipline, their own liturgical usage, and their own theological and spiritual heritage" (UR 23; cf. LG 13; AG 22). Modern conditions in the world church call for a multiple inculturation of the church in different sociocultural regions.

The unity of the church, far from being monolithic, includes a great variety of ecclesial types, oriental and occidental, having their own liturgical and spiritual traditions. If the Catholic Church were to achieve organic union with Orthodox, non-Chalcedonian, Scandinavian, or Anglican communions, there might be new ecclesial types within the one church catholic.[24] Some have tried to ground the inner diversity of the church on the doctrine of the Trinity, contending that the divine persons are distinct and mutually opposed.[25] But this line of thinking, in my judgment, is theologically unwarranted. As we have seen, all the various gifts and functions in the church come from each of the divine persons (1 Cor. 12:4–6). The diversity of functions should be christologically grounded. The church, as Christ's body, must possess different organs and members (1 Cor. 12:12–31). The Holy Spirit apportions different gifts to different groups so that the universal church may be built up in vigor and unity.

The Nairobi Assembly of the World Council of Churches in 1975 proposed a theory of Christian unity as a growing conciliar fellowship of sister churches, each of which would possess, in communion with the others, the attribute of catholicity.[26] Catholics could agree with the Nairobi Report that "true unity is not monolithic" and "does not override the special gifts given to each member and to each local church, but rather cherishes and protects them."[27] From a Catholic perspective, the problem would be to see how one could speak of true conciliarity and catholicity before the obstacles to communion had been fully overcome. In seeking true conciliar fellowship, the churches would have to confront the question of the Petrine ministry.

Conclusion

I conclude, then, that any solid ecclesiology must be rooted in the two divine processions, those of the Son and the Holy Spirit, which are continued in their respective missions. The church's visible aspect, with its personal hierarchical structures, shows forth the first mission, that of the Son (LG 8). And in its interiority the church shows forth the second mission by being the dwelling place of the Holy Spirit, who bestows his charisms and establishes the sense of interpersonal fellowship or communion. Under both aspects, the church is a sign and instrument of unity—unity among human beings of all races and nations, and between them and the Triune God. The model for the church as well as for individuals is the perfect communion among the divine persons under the "monarchy" of the Father. The body of Christ is therefore nothing other than the *Ecclesia de Trinitate*.

Christians who believe in, and are baptized in the name of, the Triune God—Father, Son, and Holy Spirit—are conjoined in a deep supernatural union. But they still fall short of the full visible unity that Christ wills for his church. By turning to the Lord of the church and humbly confessing our failures, we may be able, with God's help, to overcome the obstacles and make the church on earth prefigure more perfectly the everlasting communion of the saints in heaven.

5

The Old Testament Trinity

FREDERICA MATHEWES-GREEN

The beautiful space of Beeson's Andrew Gerow Hodges Chapel brings to mind the Scripture "Worship the LORD in the beauty of holiness" (Ps. 29:2 KJV). So many contemporary churches do not aim to be beautiful; they aim to be functional. This might still work out all right if the designers truly thought the function was worship, but too often the function is communication with the people in attendance, either teaching or entertaining or uplifting them. Hence, contemporary worship spaces look more like education spaces or entertainment arenas. This chapel was constructed to draw us into the presence of God, and it is fitting that it be beautiful, because beauty opens our hearts.

As a reporter for National Public Radio once interviewed me, she questioned this point of view: "Doesn't all the music and painting and artwork in your church distract you from focusing on God?" I replied, "Tell me this. If your husband takes you out for an anniversary dinner, and there is candlelight and roses and violins, does that distract you from feeling romantic?"

That's how humans are made, to respond to beauty with openness and joy. In this room our joy is heightened by seeing the faces of our friends: Christ, angels, and saints through history. The Romanian artist who painted it drew on ancient tradition. Last year my husband went with a mission team to Romania and saw historic churches in which paintings cover every surface, walls and ceiling, inside and out, with images from Scripture and the lives of the saints. It is an overwhelming experience, but in fact, it is the truth. These images we see are not just history-book reminders. In truth, we really *are* surrounded by a great cloud of witnesses. When we worship, they are invisibly alongside us, "in every place . . . lifting up holy hands" (1 Tim. 2:8). When we look around and see these friends surrounding us, it is as if for a moment the veil is lifted, and we see what a great company of believers we are.

Nevertheless, some things you will not see depicted here. There is an important safeguard in the tradition of Christian sacred art that keeps us from falling into idolatry. We do not make images of things that God has not shown us. We can make a painting of Christ, because he was born and walked on this earth; this human likeness is something God deliberately chose to show us, and it would be fearful superstition, if not Gnosticism, to forbid making paintings of Christ.

However, you will not see a picture of God the Father as an old man with a beard. God has not shown us that. You will not see a painting here of the Trinity. Instead, a triangle or triquetra geometrically symbolizes the Trinity.

I want to tell you about a medieval painting of the Trinity. There is one point in Scripture when God is revealed in three persons simultaneously. Can you think of what it is? No, not the baptism of Jesus—there we see Jesus, and the Holy Spirit as a dove, but only hear the voice of God. When do we see all three visibly? "The Lord appeared to [Abraham] by the oaks of Mamre, as he sat at the door of his tent in the heat of the day. He lifted up his eyes and looked, and behold, three men stood in front of him" (Gen. 18:1–2 RSV).

This painting is entitled *The Old Testament Trinity*, and is shown on the front cover of this book. It is probably the best-known and most-admired icon among Western Christians. The Russian monk Andrei Rublev painted it in 1411. People honor him as one of the most gifted icon painters. You may have seen *Andrei Rublev*, a 1966 film biography of him that was not widely released till 1987. If you did, maybe you can explain it to me, because I could not make heads or tails of it! Though most icons are anonymous—they are not signed, and usually the name of the painter is forgotten—those by Rublev have continued to bear his name because of his unusual gift. He painted with lightness, clarity, and an ethereal touch that few could equal. There is nothing sentimental about his painting, but instead a great sense of freshness.

Other renditions of this theme appear in the realm of Eastern Christian painting. Sometimes we see Abraham and Sarah in the background, holding platters of food; in that case, the title is *The Hospitality of Abraham*. This style, depicting the three figures alone, is often used on the Feast of Pentecost.

There are not many details in the image besides the commanding figures. In the background we can see an oak of Mamre; the Holy Land is such a treeless place that a stand of oaks would be a well-known landmark. The three figures sit around a stone table that early Christians would have recognized as an altar. The niche in the front represents a tomb—not only the empty tomb of Christ, but also from the time of the catacombs, the Christian custom of placing the bones of departed believers beneath their altars. On the table is a gold chalice containing red wine mixed with bread. This is how the Eastern Orthodox serve communion, by combining leavened bread and wine in the same chalice.

As we look at this icon, can we tell which is the Father, Son, or Holy Spirit? Theologians would warn us against it; distinguishing the three into separate bodies imperils the unity of the Trinity. It would be safer, perhaps, to understand that all three in combination somehow represent the Trinity together. And Genesis, it is true, does not encourage us to fix too closely on distinctions between the "three men." "They" speak to Abraham, but later it is "the Lord" who is speaking. "The men" depart, but "Abraham still stood before the Lord" (Gen. 18:22 RSV). When the company arrives in Sodom, the text no longer names "three men" nor "the Lord," but now "two angels."

Whatever is going on here, it is complicated, and Scripture does not give us enough information to sort it all out. This much we can rely on: the three men, or angels, who appear to Abraham and Sarah are a visitation from "the Lord": God has appeared to them in the form of three persons.

As I look at this icon, though, I think that Rublev intended for us to recognize three different members of the Trinity. The Father is on the left. His robe is iridescent, shifting from glowing golden-red to azure blue, a triumph of the painter's art. "You robe yourself in light as in a garment" (Ps. 104:2 author's translation). The Son and Holy Spirit both gaze toward him, inclining their heads. There is an expression of deference, reflected in the version of the Nicene Creed that Rublev would have recited daily: the Son is begotten of the Father; the Spirit proceeds from the Father. If we imagine this theology of the Trinity represented as a triangle, the point is clearly on the top. The Father is the *archē*, the source; both Son and Spirit originate in him.

I will not delve too deeply into the minutiae of history, but it was a change in European Christianity in about the ninth century that first suggested adding the term *filioque* to the Nicene Creed. This was the first appearance of the idea that the Spirit proceeds from both the Father "and the Son [*filioque*]," rather than from the Father alone. During a time when some were challenging the divinity of the Son, it seemed an appropriate safeguard to proclaim that the Son is the source of the Spirit as well. And it seemed scripturally accurate. After all, "[Jesus] breathed on them and said to them, 'Receive the Holy Spirit'" (John 20:22).

But this confuses the immediate transmission of the Spirit to humans in this world—done in this case by Jesus breathing upon his disciples—with the question of the eternal origin of the Spirit. At the beginning, the Spirit proceeds from the Father. Later, Jesus says he will ask the Father to send us the Spirit, and then he breathes on his disciples to impart the Spirit. But from before all time, the origin of the Spirit remains with the Father alone.

What do such words even mean? What does it mean that the Son is "begotten," and the Spirit "proceeds"? I am not competent to tackle such questions. "Such knowledge is too wonderful for me; it is so high that I cannot attain it" (Ps. 139:6). And when I read over the orders I received when I became a Christian, it does not look like I need to know. I just need to do my job, and prying into the deep things of God is not part of my commission. The one thing I can know is that the Father is the ultimate source, as we see here. Both Son and Spirit incline their heads to him.

The Son, in the middle, is wearing a robe of deep purple-red; this is the purple of royalty, rather than the lavender or so-called "royal purple" we think of today. Purple fabric was quite expensive; in the book of Acts (16:14), Lydia dealt in purple goods. The source of purple dye was a tiny gland at the back of the murex snail's head, and only the wealthiest could afford it; hence, it is associated with royalty. Over his purple tunic the Son wears a blue mantle, indicating divinity. Both Father and Spirit wear their blues as a tunic.

When one is looking at ancient art, one should not become too fixed on assigning symbolic meanings to colors. The artist could not just run down to the local hobby hut and buy more Blue # 3. If the seeds or minerals necessary for a color were not available or too expensive, he would have to alter the color scheme to suit what he had. Hence, some colors predominate in certain geographic areas, depending on soil and climate conditions. But in some cases, as here, we can draw some inferences about the colors used by this masterful painter.

The Spirit's green mantle, scintillating with light, is another of Rublev's achievements. Green belongs to the Spirit because he is the source of life. On the Feast of Pentecost, Eastern Orthodox churches are decorated with greenery, boughs and branches, and worshippers wear green clothing. The Orthodox prayer to the Holy Spirit begins, "O Heavenly King, Comforter, the Spirit of Truth, Who art everywhere present and fillest all things, Treasury of blessings and Giver of Life." It is this sense of the Spirit as source of life, everywhere present, filling all things, that contributes to one of the distinctives of Orthodox theology: it is intimately bound up with daily life. There is no such thing as theology that is purely intellectual. If it does not change you, if it does not flood you with light, it is not worth your time.

In the Christian East, a "theologian" is not someone who has thought hard about theological categories and labored at their construction. A theologian is someone who has drawn near God and experienced his transforming presence in a palpable way. This is what Peter means by becoming "partakers of the divine nature" (2 Pet. 1:4 KJV). A theologian is someone who has "seen the Uncreated Light," a reference to the light that shone from Jesus on Mt. Tabor (Mark 9:2–3), and which illuminated the burning bush without consuming it (Exod. 3:2). Being a theologian is akin to being a mystic—though I hate to use that word, because in the West mysticism seems like an odd calling for odd

people, while in the East it is the whole purpose of Christian
life and the calling of every person: union with God, *theōsis*. In
the fourth century Evagrius of Pontus said, "A theologian is one
whose prayer is true."

Today some of you have the job description "theologian" and
may be thinking that you did not even have plans to see the Uncreated Light. How refreshing it would be to understand your
calling as being a source of light for others, a living example of
what God can do with a fully yielded person, someone whose
deep meditation on the things of God has led to personal transformation and even holiness. That's the old meaning of the term
"theologian." Contrast this with a framed print I saw in the vest-
ing room of the National Cathedral in Washington. It showed
a shining candle surrounded by darkness, and the text read: "I
was wandering all alone in a dark forest, with only the light of
a single candle to guide me, and along came a theologian and
blew it out."

Son and Spirit, as I said, both bow their heads to the Father.
But all three show equality in other ways. Each of them carries
a slim red staff, an emblem of authority. Each has a halo, which
we should not understand as a flat disk behind the head, but
as a globe of light encircling the head, like the sphere around a
candle flame. All three gesture toward the chalice with their right
hands; the Father and the Son hold their fingers in the form of
a blessing. Though I have been referring to the three figures as
Father, Son, and Spirit, you will notice that they all look alike.
Rublev does not depict the Son in the familiar likeness of Jesus.
This visitation to Abraham took place many centuries before
the incarnation. Instead, Rublev has relied on the indication
in Genesis that the three resembled angels, and so he depicts
them in the way angels usually appear in iconography: as young
men with long, curly hair pulled back, no beards, and delicate
gold wings.

Notice, too, what Rublev has done with perspective in the
painting. The top of the table, and the tops of the pedestals the
Father and Spirit rest their feet upon, tilt toward us dramatically,
as if we are looking down on the scene from above. At the level
of the figures' faces, however, we seem to be looking at them
directly from about shoulder height. This was not a matter of
incompetence. A painter who can handle drapery and color as

well as Rublev does is not ignorant of the method of perspective. It is intentional. As is often the case in iconography, the artist has distorted perspective in order to give us a sensation that the scene is bursting out toward us, with the chalice in the center pressing itself our way.

In conventional painting we expect things to grow smaller as they go into the distance, till they reach "the vanishing point." From elementary school art class we remember that as the railroad tracks go away from us, far in the distance they converge. Yet icons often play with reversing or distorting perspective in order to increase the viewer's sense of being off-balance in an unfamiliar, powerful world, or even to feel that the whole scene is rushing toward one, converging on one in a challenging way. An artist may carefully arrange a painting so that everything becomes larger as the scene goes back, and smaller in the foreground, so that the vanishing point is right about where the viewer is standing. Thus we, the viewers, are the vanishing point; if God did not sustain us, we would vanish.

A symposium on a complex theological topic like the Trinity runs a danger of dryness, and I wanted to offer a bit of refreshment by focusing on a beautiful example of ancient Christian art, and seeing how it can be an aid to devotion, to greater openness to God. This is where my story ends. Everything we are doing over these few days should be enhancing our devotion. We should all be on the way to becoming theologians. A large gathering can nurture fellowship and deepen faith, but it is also an opportunity for the devil to stir up trouble, by stimulating pride or by dashing pride, by undermining self-confidence, or by stirring up a craving to dominate others.

So "take every thought captive to obey Christ" (2 Cor. 10:5) and examine yourselves, taking care that you not be led astray. The evil one comes only to steal, kill, and destroy, and he is indisputably prowling around, seeking whom he may devour (1 Pet. 5:8). Let your conversations, in public and private, be seasoned with salt. We are surrounded by a great cloud of witnesses; we see them visibly in this dome, but they also are invisibly with us, in the eternal company of angels and all who love the Lord. That is where we are all going, and when we arrive there, we will have to give an account for every careless word we utter. So let us plan ahead for that, and watch our words now. When in doubt, silence is a good option. Because, after all we have said about this icon today, there is one thing we have not yet recognized: none of the figures are speaking. The tranquility of their silence is sufficient. During this conference I hope you have opportunity to spend some time in similar silence, and thus enter further into the mystery of the Trinity.

6

A Puritan Perspective

Trinitarian Godliness according to John Owen

J. I. PACKER

I want you to meet one of my most honored traveling companions over the past fifty-five years, the English Puritan John Owen, who lived from 1616 to 1683. To many moderns his name means nothing, but in his day he was a quite distinguished man. During the 1650s he became chaplain and adviser to Oliver Cromwell, and was made dean of Christ Church, Oxford's largest college, and also vice-chancellor of the university. Through the years of persecution that the Restoration ushered in, when nonconforming clergy and congregations risked fines and imprisonment for worshipping God their way, Owen led the Congregationalists, pastored a gathered church, and constantly sought toleration for all orthodox believers.[1] He died before toleration came.

Owen's abiding legacy is a series of what are, by common consent of those who know them, classic treatments of major themes of the Christian faith and the Christian life, affirming Reformed

Christianity and vindicating it against Roman, Arminian, and Socinian alternatives. Specifically, Owen wrote on bibliology,[2] the history of revelation,[3] Christology,[4] the Holy Spirit,[5] justification by faith,[6] the church,[7] communion with God,[8] sin and mortification,[9] the saints' perseverance and assurance, and apostasy.[10] He also authored a huge exposition of Hebrews, which fills seven of the twenty-four volumes in Goold's edition of his works and is a veritable treasure-house of covenant theology and devotion.[11] Owen's readers have always marveled at the structural solidity, scriptural soundness, weight, and warmth of these writings; I confess myself one of that number, and I do not wonder that in conversation, long ago now, Professor Roger Nicole rated Owen the greatest of English theologians.

Yet, enriching as he is, it is not easy for a reader to come to terms with Owen's writings. There are at least three reasons for this.

First, his literary style is formidable. Historic Puritanism took on board two contrasting ideals of style, both seemingly based on classical models. The style of Tacitus and Seneca was terse, jabbing, and pointed, with short sentences in short paragraphs. The style of Cicero and Quintilian was complex, flowing, argumentative, with long sentences, many subordinate clauses, rhetorical displacements, long paragraphs. Many who were primarily preachers, like Richard Sibbes and Thomas Watson, embraced the former style; some who were primarily scholars chose the second path, like Owen, and the classicist-turned-pamphleteer John Milton, just as, back in Elizabeth's day, Richard Hooker had done. Hooker and Milton achieve real eloquence in this idiom, but literary grace, as distinct from clear and solid reasoning, was beyond Owen's powers. At his best, Owen becomes stately; that is the height of his stylistic achievement; at his worst, he is simply cumbersome. Almost all the time, he is long-winded and slow-moving, and what he writes always feels like thinking done in Latin and put into English at the last minute, while his use of archaic words and word forms—archaic even to him, like "withal" for "with"—though clearly meant to add weight to what he says, actually only adds to the roughness of the reading. (Note though that Owen's is more of a spoken style than at first appears, and his essential lucidity always breaks surface when one reads him aloud.)

Second, Owen's mind-set is formidable, too. In him we see great learning, a great sense of the teacher's responsibility to be thorough, a lawyer's passion for leaving no stone unturned in argument, an unquenchable urge for exactness of statement, and a personal reserve that led him to a dignified formality of utterance on every occasion. Queen Victoria complained that Gladstone always spoke to her as if she were a public meeting, and something of that pomposity also appears in Owen. Thus, on the day of his death, when a pastor friend visiting the invalid told him that his final work, *Meditations and Discourses on the Glory of Christ*, was now in the press, Owen replied: "I am glad to hear it; but O brother Payne! the long wished for day has come at last, in which I shall see that glory in another manner than I have ever done, or was capable of doing, in this world." Eloquent, certainly, as Sinclair Ferguson says;[12] but it is an unusual person who talks like that when he feels he is dying.

Yet it would be quite wrong to conclude that because Owen never wore his heart on his sleeve, but spoke and wrote in a formal and sententious way all the time, he was really cold and distant and perhaps somewhat hollow inside.[13] The following extended extract, from the closing admonitory section of the thirty-thousand-word preface to the refutation of Socinianism that the government had commissioned him to write, enables us to monitor the true heartbeat of this extraordinary man of God.

> When the heart is cast indeed into the mould of the doctrine that the mind embraceth; when the evidence and necessity of the truth abides in us; when not the sense of the words only is in our heads, but the sense of the things abides in our hearts; when we have communion with God in the doctrine we contend for,—then shall we be garrisoned, by the grace of God, against all the assaults of men. And without this all our contending, as to ourselves, is of no value. What am I the better if I can dispute that Christ is God, but have no sense of sweetness in my heart from hence that he is a God in covenant with my soul? What will it avail me to evince, by testimonies and arguments, that he hath made satisfaction for sin, if, through my unbelief, the wrath of God abideth on me, and I have no experience of my own being made the righteousness of God in him,—if I find not, in my standing before God, the excellency of having my sins imputed to him and his righteousness

imputed to me? Will it be any advantage to me, in the issue, to profess and dispute that God works the conversion of a sinner by the irresistible grace of his Spirit, if I was never acquainted experimentally with the deadness and utter impotency to good, that opposition to the law of God, which is in my own soul by nature, and with the efficacy of the exceeding greatness of the power of God in quickening, enlightening, and bringing forth the fruits of obedience in me? It is the power of truth in the heart alone that will make us cleave unto it indeed in an hour of temptation. Let us, then, not think we are any thing the better for our conviction of the truths of the great doctrines of the gospel . . . unless we find the power of the truths abiding in our own hearts, and have a continual experience of their necessity and excellency in our standing before God and our communion with him.[14]

As this shows, it is integral to Owen's mind-set to insist that experiencing the power of gospel truth is essential. Though he was not chatty about his spiritual pilgrimage in the way that Augustine and Luther and Baxter and Bunyan were, we must not therefrom infer that he stood aloof from this characteristic Puritan conviction and commitment. Says he:

I hope I may own in sincerity, that my heart's desire unto God, and the chief design of my life in the station wherein the good providence of God hath placed me [as vice-chancellor of Oxford University], is that mortification and universal holiness may be promoted in my own and in the hearts and ways of others, to the glory of God.[15]

We should not doubt that he meant what he said.

The third and final reason why it is hard to tune in to Owen is his confusing expository style. He has a habit of dividing topics under two or three subheads, which then themselves may be subdivided and subsubdivided too. This procedure, however, is typically Puritan; it is the fault not of an individual, but of a culture; what it shows is the influence of Ramist theory, which prescribed the dichotomizing of concepts—subdividing them into pairs, and splitting those pairs into more pairs, and so on—as being the key to epistemological and educational mastery of all realities.[16] Ramus was a French Protestant killed in the Bartholomew's Day massacre of 1572; his ideas had much influence in the Puritan heyday. Anyhow, a pattern of subheads really does make for thoroughness of coverage and clarity of grasp in educational enterprises generally. But Owen burdens our minds by giving us too much of this good thing. Yet those who use pencil and paper as they read, to chart the subdivisions they meet, will soon find themselves following the flow of Owen's logic without difficulty, so that they no longer feel that his layout is a problem. (Please receive this as my challenge to the Reader, in a rather different sense from that of the young Ellery Queen!)

Owen's Theology

How did John Owen understand his role and tasks as a theologian? To answer this question means querying some familiar perspectives, so let us prepare our minds to make adjustments.

First, Owen lived before the concept of a theologian was scaled down to its current, intellectualized, and relatively narrow dimensions. Two centuries ago Enlightenment thinkers set up the curriculum for theological students in universities and seminaries as consisting of four distinct fields of inquiry: history and exegesis of the Bible, analysis of the church's beliefs, church history, and ministerial practice. The new thing in this arrangement, the separation of these studies from each other, opened the door to specialization, which has been acidly but not unfairly described as getting to know more and more about less and less. Specialization produced exegetes who were not theologians, dogmaticians who were not exegetes, church historians who were neither dogmaticians nor exegetes, and practical theologians to whom past patterns of Christian life and pastoral care were a closed book. Unity was lost, fragmentation set in, and theology as a study came to mean no more than exploring facts and arguments in any or all of these departments from some personal standpoint or other, never mind what. This, of course, exactly fulfilled the freethinking intellectual ideal of the Enlightenment. Today we children of the Enlightenment are so used to it that we can hardly believe mainstream Christians ever thought of theological study differently.[17] But they did.

From the first Christian centuries down to, and past, Owen's day, people conceived of theology as wisdom and in personal rather than academic terms: that is, as the wisdom of those in whose head and heart, through the power of God's Word and Spirit, true understanding of God's revealed truth had taken root. The idea of a theologian was of a wise, godly pundit. Gregory Nazianzus and John Calvin were both called "the theologian" in their own lifetime, and in each case the title meant all of the above. On this view, real theologians embodied the unity of thought and modeled the reality of worship, obedience, and care that together amount to what the Bible means by *knowing God*. They would use exegesis to buttress their exposition of the faith; their exegesis would reflect, and responsibly relate to, their believing state of mind. They would read historical theology as narrating the wars of the Word in and with the world, and church history as recording successes and failures in faithfulness to the gospel. The application of truth to life would be their constant concern. Intellectually and attitudinally, the theologian's wisdom would thus be a single ball of wax, the product of all the disciplines of divinity and devotion operating together in one man's life. In this sense John Owen aimed to be, and truly was, a theologian.

Next, we should recognize that Owen was a respected Puritan theologian of typically Reformed convictions. Appreciating this may once again show us that we need to adjust some of our conventional assumptions.

Focus first on Owen's Puritan identity. The Puritans of popular fancy, as we know, were a rigid, bigoted lot; obsessive about sin and fixated on hell; sworn foes of pleasure, laughter, and art; boors, sourpusses, and killjoys; and in many cases holier-than-thou hypocrites. Say "Puritan," and people think at once of Shakespeare's Malvolio, a character whose cartoon name proclaims ill will and tells us at once that he has been created simply in order to receive a comic comeuppance. They think too of Hawthorne's Arthur Dimmesdale, a nineteenth-century romantic antihero placed in a seventeenth-century costume drama. But whatever individual bad apples may have intruded into the Puritan barrel, the great body of those in the movement were not in the least like those fictional figures. Led by gifted and godly clergy with stellar pastoral records, the Puritans of English history were a holiness movement at the personal and family level, a renewal and reform movement in the church, and an energizing force for justice and against abuse of privilege in the nation at every level. From the 1560s to the 1660s, through what has been called the Puritan century, it was the Puritans who made things run in England's religious life. Those Puritans who colonized America from the 1620s onward managed to maintain the English ideal as New England's accepted standard for more than a century and a half.

The Puritans formed a Bible-based, Christ-centered, conversionist, devotional, church-related, and community-oriented movement. The temper of Puritan religion was practical, experiential, conscientious, determined, hopeful, prayerful, and hardworking. These Christians sought sanctity in all circumstances, personal states and relationships, walks of life and activities, both at home and abroad. For the Puritan, everything everywhere in every respect must become a specific instance of holiness to the Lord. Arguably, Puritanism represents the most complete, profound, mature, and magnificent realization of biblical religion that the world has yet seen, one that few since the seventeenth century have matched and none have surpassed. But be that as it may, it was this Puritanism that from start to finish was John Owen's personal way of life.

Now consider Owen's Reformed identity. About this, at a surface level, there is no secret and no dispute. Owen made his name by his *Display of Arminianism* (1642) and *The Death of Death in the Death of Christ* (1648).[18] Throughout his career he was affirming the famous "five points" of the Synod of Dordt against Roman Catholic, Arminian, and Socinian demurrers, and others were honoring him as a bastion of Calvinistic orthodoxy. But what does that mean? The Calvinism of popular fancy, and of much academic fancy too till quite recently,[19] is a relatively simplistic, monolithic, and actually rationalistic viewpoint. It starts with the thought of God's absolute sovereignty in creation, providence, and grace, and then supposedly deduces from that a kind of logical iron maiden (or Procrustean bed, or jelly mold, if you prefer a gentler image) into which all biblical doctrines are then pressed. At every point it emphasizes the decisiveness of divine decision and action while dismissing human decision and action as unimportant. But this is a caricature both of Calvin and of those who came after him in the Reformed succession.

The truth is that Reformation and Puritan theologians saw themselves as pastoral persons engaged in a recovery movement for the health of the church and the salvation of souls. They saw the church's biblical faith as being like the mainstream of a flowing river, with eddies, backwaters, and muddy pools at its edge, out of the central flow. By purging and renewing that faith as they found it, and establishing a pattern of faithfully teaching it, they believed that they were piloting the church back from the edge, where it had drifted from the mainstream. And then they must be on guard lest the church drift again, making further recovery work necessary. To do their job, therefore, they needed both to chart the true main flow, which meant interacting with the entire Bible and the whole history of Christian thought, and to controvert any errors that threatened to mislead the church in their own day.

So Carl Trueman, in his fine book subtitled *John Owen's Trinitarian Theology*,[20] is entirely correct in writing:

> To seventeenth-century Reformed theologians, Calvin's writings are one (admittedly important) resource among many, alongside which must be placed not only other Reformed writers but also the works of the Fathers and the medieval schoolmen. Those who think they have understood Owen and his Puritan contemporaries simply in terms of the Reformed tradition of the sixteenth and seventeenth centuries have not really understood him at all. Other branches of the Western tradition also play vital roles in his theological work, and to ignore, generalize about, or dismiss these on the basis of aprioristic prejudices about Scholasticism, medieval theology etc. is to do a fundamental injustice to the work of a highly sophisticated thinker. . . . He was throughout his theological career engaging in a critical interaction with, and appropriation of, the Western tradition as a whole.[21]

That is the kind of theologian that John Owen was.

In his theological writing, Owen shows himself a fully integrated thinker, whose mind holds together disciplines, perspectives, emphases, and concerns that the modern church and its modern evangelicals too often disjoin and keep separate. It will help us now to review some of the key conjunctions that give Owen's work its unity and overall shape. As Carl Trueman says, Owen belongs within the

> developing tradition of European Reformed Orthodoxy that included Dordt and Westminster. . . . His theology reflects the broad

parameters and concerns of the Reformed tradition: a high view of Scripture as the epistemological basis of theology; an understanding of salvation rooted in the divine covenants; an historical economy of salvation focused on the person and work of the Lord Jesus Christ; and a basic concern to bring out the Trinitarian nature of God's creative and saving activity.[22]

Within this frame, we should recognize several features. Owen offers expositions that are both systematic and exegetical, in which he always confirms and illustrates affirmations of dogma from biblical texts. In spelling out God's relation to his world and to humankind within it, he distinguishes first and second causes in the manner of the Westminster Confession (6.2): "Although, in relation to the foreknowledge and decree of God, the first cause, all things come to pass immutably, and infallibly; yet, by the same providence, he ordereth them to fall out, according to the nature of second causes, either necessarily, freely, or contingently."[23] This gives responsive human decision Godward its true significance alongside initiating divine decision humanward. Owen thus shows what it means to say that God has both made us and redeemed us for fellowship with himself in love, fellowship that we freely and wholeheartedly choose.

In line with this, Owen constantly shows us both his academic and his pastoral side, analyzing and defending truths with formidable technical competence and applying them in a most searching and powerful way—with unction, one has to say—to his readers' consciences. "Unction" means the power of the Holy Spirit on human words, spoken and written. At this distance we cannot tell with what unction Owen spoke in public, but few can ever have matched him for unction on the written word when he addresses the heart. He alternates between the doctrinal and the devotional in work after work, teaching truth and practice with equal facility and force. Rigorously objective and formal in stating biblical truths, he becomes deeply personal and relational as he uses them to evoke response to the God who speaks them to us and through them calls us to the obedience of faith. Owen has an equal passion for orthodoxy, the codifying of all that God has revealed, and for orthopraxy, the godliness that comes from taking revealed truth truly to heart. He is equally anxious that all we think, say, and do should be doxological, glorifying God, and transformational, changing us through the Holy Spirit's power toward ever-increasing Christlikeness, which yet in this life is always patchy, partial, and incomplete. And he displays equal concern and care that the full trinitarian faith of orthodoxy should lead to full trinitarian communion with God in experience. This theme occupies us directly for the rest of this presentation.

Owen on Communion with God

In a broad sense, all of Owen's writings on the Christian life are exploring the realities of communion with God, but our center of reference is and must be his work published in 1658, whose full title is *Of Communion with the Father, Son, and Holy Ghost, Each Person Distinctly, in Love, Grace, and Consolation; or, The Saints' Fellowship with the Father, Son, and Holy Ghost Unfolded.*[24] It presents the enlarged substance of sermons preached some years earlier. Its proportions—5 pages on the meaning of communion, 24 on communion with the Father, 182 on communion with the Son, and 52 on communion with the Spirit—prepare us to find it ungainly and not well shaped. For all that, as Daniel Burgess says in his foreword, it surely contains "the very highest of angels' food, . . . manna to sound Christians."[25] To appreciate its thrust and contents fully, we need to see it in relation to other elements of Owen's thought, which here Owen takes for granted, and I let that fact determine the following presentation.

First, then, we acknowledge Owen's view of how important the truth of the Trinity is. To him it is, quite simply, the foundation of Christianity, which collapses without it. The gospel of salvation through a divine-human mediator and a divine Spirit cannot be true if trinitarianism is false, nor can there then be such a thing as communion with the three persons of the Godhead distinctly. But trinitarianism is not false. Set forth in Scripture in terms that to Owen's mind are too clear to be evaded, the doctrine of the Trinity in essence is this: "that *God is one*; that this one God is *Father, Son, and Holy Ghost*; that *the Father is the Father of the Son*; and *the Son, the Son of the Father*; and *the Holy Ghost, the Spirit of the Father and the Son*; and that, in respect of their mutual relations, they are distinct from each other."[26] The proto-

Unitarian Socinians—who denied the Trinity by mishandling the relevant Scriptures, adopted a Pelagian idea of self-salvation by following Jesus, and substituted that self-salvation for the biblical gospel of sovereign grace—were thus Christianity's most mortal foes.

From 1654, when Owen accepted the Council of State's directive to write a refutation of the recently published catechism of the English Socinian John Biddle,[27] he had the threat of Socinianism constantly in his mind. Witness to this is his *Vindication of the Doctrine of the Trinity* (1669), his full-scale celebrations in print of the person and work of the Holy Spirit (*Pneumatologia*, 1674) and of the incarnate mediator (*Christologia*, 1677; and *The Glory of Christ*, 1684), and much interactive byplay in his four folio volumes on Hebrews (1668, 1674, 1680, 1684). For Owen, the truth of the Trinity is basic, crucial, and totally nonnegotiable.

Second, we observe Owen's understanding of the trinitarian structure of God's plan of salvation. Rooted in the ultimate mystery of God's sovereignty and love, the plan began with what Owen and his peers called the covenant of redemption. In light of explicit statements in John's Gospel[28] (to look no further), they conceived this reality as an eternal consensus between the Father and the Son. Thereby the Father appointed the Son to become incarnate and—as prophet, priest, and king—to mediate salvation to a great multitude of sinners. He did this through his atoning death in humiliation on the cross, his exaltation from the grave to the glory of the celestial throne, and his joining the Father in sending the Spirit to bring salvation home to blinded and twisted human hearts. Depending upon the covenant of redemption was the covenant of grace, whereby God established a new relationship of pardon, acceptance, adoption, and protection, through Christ the mediator, with sinners whom the Spirit had led to faith and repentance. On this similarly nonnegotiable substance of doctrine, communion with God rests, according to Owen.

Third, we recognize Owen's understanding of communion itself. Today, "communion with God" is a fuzzy phrase that often means no more than feeling close to God, however conceived, but otherwise it lacks specific content. Owen, however, has a much more precise notion, which the Greek word *koinōnia* in itself and as used in the New Testament abundantly warrants. The root idea of *koinōnia* is sharing through give and take, which in terms of New Testament religion means take and give. So Owen defines communion generically as "the mutual communication of such good things as wherein the persons holding that communion are delighted, bottomed upon some union between them." He defines communion with God specifically as "his *communication of himself unto us, with our returnal unto him* of that which he requireth and accepteth, flowing from that *union* which in Jesus Christ we have with him."[29]

What we receive from God, says Owen, is the love of the Father, the grace of the Son (grace both personal and purchased, as Owen analyzes it), and the life-transforming grace of the Holy Spirit—three realities overlapping in a way that shows them to be three aspects of the one reality of the Triune God's saving goodness in election, redemption, and transformation. The distinction on which distinct communion with each of the Holy Three is based is not distinction of blessings, but distinction of roles, or distinguishable primacy of action, within the solidarity of divine saving activity. The classic doctrine of appropriations ascribes creation to the Father, redemption to the Son, and new creation to the Spirit, on the basis that all three are invariably together in all the divine doings. Owen thus endorses a medieval maxim: *Omnia opera Trinitatis ad extra indivisa sunt.* On this basis Owen distinguishes the Father communicating grace as salvation's loving originator, the Son communicating it as salvation's loving achiever, and the Spirit communicating it as salvation's loving imparter. He expresses this by saying that "the Father doth it"—communicates grace—"by the way of *original* [originating] *authority*; the Son by way of communicating from a *purchased treasury*; the Holy Spirit by the way of *immediate efficacy*."[30] Owen devotes the entire treatise to working out this thought by means of cumulative exposition that shows it to be the consistent biblical way of thinking.

Fourth, at this point we need to honor Owen's view of spiritual understanding as the basic element in faith; otherwise, his account of faith-fellowship with the three divine persons will remain opaque to us. Already it is clear that he is not expounding any form of mysticism, whereby a person in an unmediated flight transcends to the ineffable. Nor has he in mind any form of immediate private revelation of or about or from any of the three persons that would take the devoted soul beyond the range of criticism or censure. And he is far away from the apophatic mode of theology, which deprecates ratiocination because God is beyond our full grasp, and then turns to allegory as an alternative. But in speaking about communion with God, Owen takes for granted that the Holy Spirit has already illuminated our hearts. Hence, the Holy Spirit has overcome the blindness to divine things that our innate depravity has induced, and the Christian will now acknowledge what the Bible sets forth as reality. Owen's doctrine, largely set forth in his various writings, is that as part of the process of regeneration the Spirit gives *light*: power, that is, to perceive the spiritual order to which Scripture testifies. With that, the Spirit implants a habit of love for God's truth and resistance to sinful ways of thinking. Without all this, a person will know only biblical notions and will be found disagreeing with many of them. Through this, however, the Christian will receive as solid fact all that Scripture reveals about God, and the heart will cleave to what the mind now apprehends. So Trueman writes:

> In line with the Reformed emphasis upon the inseparability of knowledge of God and true piety, Owen's view of human cognition has a vital practical direction. As the mind is enabled to grasp God in his revelation, so it inclines the will and affections to be obedient to him. Faith, then, can never be construed as *mere* intellectual assent, because intellectual assent is always more than that, leading as it does to an act of the will. . . . Owen is clearly developing a notion of theology as a habit.[31]

This returns us to the personal conception of the theologian's identity, to which I referred earlier.

According to John Owen, communion with God is a subset of knowledge of God through Word and Spirit, according to the teaching of the apostle Paul, and after Paul follows John Calvin, and then the Reformed theologians, of whom Owen is one. We are now able to state the personal and relational aspects of this communion with some precision. By faith, through the open eyes of the heart as explained above, the Christian contemplates the living God in the pages of the Bible, knowing that this God in his triunity is the same yesterday, today, and forever, and is present as the immediate environment of everyone's ongoing life. The

Christian therefore prays and obeys, practicing God's presence as a discipline of the heart and making God's honor and glory a constant goal. When praying, the Christian speaks to the God he knows is there, thanking and praising him for his grace and goodness, claiming his promises and trusting his faithfulness to them. The Christian is begging for help in the battle against the world and the flesh and the devil, loving God in return for his love, hoping in him, rejoicing in him, and celebrating the privilege and security of being his adopted child. Then in obedience the Christian labors to run in the way of God's commandments, honoring and pleasing him as fully as possible in every activity of life. Such is the personal and relational dimension of communion with God, which Owen, following Scripture as he understands it, spells out in relation to each of the three divine persons in turn.

Within this frame we set our survey of Owen's exposition. We begin with its centerpiece, the more than two-thirds of it that is devoted to communion with Jesus Christ the mediator. The seeming disproportion reflects Owen's view of the Christ-centeredness of the Bible itself, and of the proper prominence of the mediator in both Christian theology and Christian devotion. Declaring that communion with Jesus Christ our Lord is in grace, according to the familiar benediction of 2 Corinthians 13:13–14, Owen dwells in turn on Christ's *"personal presence and comeliness,"* the adorable adequacy and beauty that the Savior displays, and on what he calls the *"purchased grace"* of the Christian's new relationship with God by virtue of the Savior's obedient life, atoning death, and heavenly intercession. The thoughts intertwine and are helped along by extended exposition of the Canticles, which, conventionally for his day, Owen reads as an allegory (parable, I think, would be the better word) of "conjugal affection" between Christians and their Lord, a bond issuing in "(1) *Sweetness.* (2) *Delight.* (3) *Safety.* (4) *Comfort, . . . supportment and consolation."*[32] Pursuing this, Owen strikingly expounds the "loveliness" of Christ by declaring him:

> Lovely in his *person*,—in the glorious all-sufficiency of his Deity, gracious purity and holiness of his humanity, authority and majesty, love and power.

Lovely in his *birth* and incarnation; when he was rich, for our sakes becoming poor. . . .

Lovely in the whole course of his life, and the more than angelical holiness and obedience which, in the depth of poverty and persecution, he exercised therein;—doing good, receiving evil; blessing, and being cursed, reviled, reproached, all his days.

Lovely in his *death*; yea, therein most lovely to sinners;—never more glorious and desirable than when he came broken, dead, from the cross. Then had he carried all our sins into a land of forgetfulness; then had he made peace and reconciliation for us. . . .

Lovely in his whole *employment*, in his great undertaking,—in his *life, death, resurrection, ascension*; being a mediator between God and us, to recover the glory of God's justice, and to save our souls,—to bring us to an enjoyment of God. . . .

Lovely in the glory and majesty wherewith he is *crowned*. Now he is set down at the right hand of the Majesty on high; where, though he be terrible to his enemies, yet he is full of mercy, love, and compassion, towards his beloved ones.

Lovely in all those *supplies of grace and consolations*, in all the dispensations of his Holy Spirit, whereof his saints are made partakers.

Lovely in all the *tender care, power, and wisdom*, which he exercises in the protection, safe-guarding, and delivery of his church and people, in the midst of all the oppositions and persecutions whereunto they are exposed.

Lovely in all his *ordinances*, and the whole of that spiritually glorious worship which he has appointed to his people, whereby they draw nigh and have communion with him and his Father.

Lovely and glorious in the *vengeance* he taketh, and will finally execute, upon the stubborn enemies of himself and his people.

Lovely in the *pardon* he hath purchased and doth dispense,—in the reconciliation he hath established,—in the grace he communicates,—in the consolation he doth administer,—in the peace and joy he gives his saints, in his assured preservation of them unto glory.

What shall I say? there is no end of his excellencies and desirableness;—"He is altogether lovely. This is our beloved, and this is our friend, O daughters of Jerusalem."[33]

There is much more in the same vein.

Of communion with the Father and the Spirit, Owen says less, and I need say less here. Communion with the Father means receiving the biblical witness to his fatherly love in Christ for all believers in Christ, and responding by resting in him with constant delight, through all the ups and downs of daily providence and all the particular disciplinary dispensations that come our way.[34] "So shall we walk in the light of God's countenance, and hold holy communion with our Father all the day long."[35] "Exercise your thoughts upon . . . the eternal, free, and fruitful love of the Father, and see if your hearts be not wrought upon to delight in him. I dare boldly say, believers will find it as thriving a course as ever they pitched on in their lives."[36]

Communion with the Holy Spirit fulfills the fellowship pattern of receiving and responding in a directly experiential way. First, we recognize what his work in our lives, as the sanctifying indweller, is giving us: teaching, in the double sense of Christ-centered instruction from Scripture and illumination to understand it; comfort, whereby our spirits are raised and our hearts encouraged; assurance of the love of the Father and the Son toward us, and therein of his own love too; character change into his own likeness, which is the image of Christ and of the Father;[37] marking us out for God and giving us foretastes of heaven's joy. There is a self-evidencing immediacy in the Spirit's openings and applications to us of what is written: "When the Holy Ghost . . . stills the tumults and storms that are raised in the soul, giving it an immediate calm and security, it knows his divine power, and rejoices in his presence."[38] And there is a foretaste of the life of heaven in this, as Owen brings out in his comments on the gift of the Spirit as an earnest of our inheritance (2 Cor. 1:22; 5:5; Eph. 1:14): "That a thing be an earnest, it is required,—(1) That it be part of the whole, *of the same kind* and nature with it. . . . (2) That it be a *confirmation of a promise*. . . . So is he [the Spirit] in all respects completely an earnest,—given of God, received by us, as the beginning of our inheritance, and the assurance of it. So much as we have of the Spirit, so much we have of heaven in perfect enjoyment, and so much evidence of its future fullness."[39]

What then is our proper response to the Spirit's ministry? This is formulated throughout, as you will notice, in theological parallel to our due response to Christ:

The Scripture so fully, frequently, clearly, distinctly ascribing the things we have been speaking of to the immediate efficacy of the Holy

Ghost, faith closeth with him in the truth revealed, and peculiarly regards him, worships him, serves him, waits for him, prayeth to him, praiseth him. . . . Herein have we communion and fellowship with him. . . . Doth he shed abroad the love of God in our hearts? Doth he witness unto our adoption? The soul considers his presence, ponders his love, his condescension, goodness, and kindness; is filled with reverence of him, and cares [takes care] not to grieve him, and labours to preserve his temple, his habitation, pure and holy. . . .

When we feel our hearts warmed with joy, supported in peace, established in our obedience, let us ascribe to him the praise that is due to him. . . . Glorifying of the Holy Ghost in thanksgivings . . . is no small part of our communion with him. . . . There is no duty that leaves a more heavenly savour in the soul than this doth. . . .

Humbling *ourselves for our miscarriages* in reference to him is another part of our communion with him. That we have *grieved* him as to his person, *quenched* him as to the motion of his grace, or *resisted* him in his ordinances, is to be mourned for.[40]

We can now see why Amy Plantinga Pauw, in part following Janice Knight,[41] counted Owen, this greatest of Puritan theologians, along with Richard Sibbes, John Cotton, and Thomas Goodwin as "Spiritual Brethren,"[42] all majoring on a trinitarian model of the Christian life. She distinguishes them from Puritanism's "Intellectual Fathers," Perkins, Ames, Hooker, Shepard, John Winthrop, and Peter Bulkeley—though failing to list Owen as an Intellectual Father of Puritanism just because he was a spiritual brother does seem a bit odd.[43] Be that as it may, Owen does here work out the experiential intimacy of Christian devotion Godward in strictly trinitarian terms, and he did consistently maintain this perspective throughout his theological career.[44]

Conclusions

Here, then, in a nutshell we have John Owen's fully and even radically trinitarian account of the inside story of Christian existence. My personal admiration for it will be obvious from the way I have presented it, but that is not what I want to dwell on as I close. Rather, I underline four features of the account itself.

First, observe that Owen builds a social view of the existence and unity of God into his writings. Already implicit in the Reformed axiom that the eternal covenant of redemption is the linchpin of God's saving action, this feature, equally integral to the trinitarian thought of both the Cappadocians and Augustine, is increasingly becoming integral to Christian thought about God today. After two centuries of virtual Unitarianism in the main academic stream, at least among Protestants, this is something for which we should be quite thankful.

Second, observe that by exact attention to biblical statements—more exact than I have been able adequately to illustrate—Owen achieves an equal honoring of the three divine persons in a way that Reformed theology, Father-fixated as it tends to be, has not always done. Charismatic theology, Spirit-fixated as it tends to be in reaction against what Barth somewhere called "flat-tire" Christianity, has not done much better. Surely, however, equal honoring of the three persons is the way God's people should always go.

Third, observe Owen's assumption that thought control—leading to well-ordered beliefs, meditations, soliloquies, and prayers—is a habit that all Christians as such can and should develop. Here, again, is something I wish I could have illustrated more fully. Belief in the primacy of the intellect is basic to Owen's anthropology, and he is clearly convinced that for the regenerate to be thinking constantly and consistently about the Triune God, whom they love and desire beyond all other realities, is both possible and natural. What some would dismiss as barren Reformed intellectualism, Owen sees as the path to Christian maturity, and surely with reason.

Fourth, observe Owen's assumption that all Christians, not just a brainy few, do need and benefit from meticulous expository theology. As editor Goold points out, it is likely that the sermons out of which Owen builds the treatise *Of Communion* first "refreshed and cheered" his congregation at rural Coggeshall,[45] where he was minister before moving to Ireland and then to Oxford. Meticulous expository theology is all that Owen ever offered to any congregation; he believed that this was every Christian's true food.

So now I end with two questions: What difference would it make to the evangelicalism we are used to, and the evangelical piety that I trust we all labor to practice, if into the mix we fed Owen's emphases on theology, theologians, and communion with God? Would we favor that? I wonder!

7

The Trinity and the Challenge of Islam

Timothy George

At Oxford University is a gigantic painting of a man and a small boy by the sea. The painting is based on a story told about the great Augustine, Bishop of Hippo, who was writing his famous book *De Trinitate*, the greatest classic, perhaps, ever written on the subject of the Trinity. As the story goes, Augustine was walking along the coast one day when he met a small boy pouring seawater into a hole in the ground. Augustine watched him for some time and eventually asked him what he was doing. "I'm pouring the Mediterranean Sea into this hole," replied the boy. "Don't be so stupid," admonished Augustine. "You can't fit the sea into that little hole. You're wasting your time." "And so are you," the boy shot back, "trying to write a book on God!" We smile at that story, and yet we recognize the profundity and the truth that it conveys. The admonition to reticence and humility in talking about the Trinity is essential because no one is able to grasp completely and to comprehend fully the reality of the one God who is the Father, the Son, and the Holy Spirit. And yet, as Augustine also said, we say "three persons" not in order to say something, but in order not to be silent in the face of such mystery.

Vincent of Lèrins was a contemporary of Augustine and died around 450, about twenty years after Augustine. We best remember him because of what we call the Vincentian Canon. This statement summarizes the consensual wisdom of the ancient church, East and West, in a famous line: "That which is believed always, everywhere, and by everybody." Nevertheless, anyone with even a minimum historical knowledge of Christian theology would have difficulty in naming many things that fit this requirement. We may even ask, "Does Vincent of Lèrins's statement apply to anything in Christian thinking?" If there is anything at all, then surely it ought to be the doctrine of the Holy Trinity. In this volume we have, from quite different perspectives, some sense of a common foundational affirmation about the reality of God, the Holy Trinity: the Father, the Son, and the Holy Spirit.

In this essay, I explore the Trinity and the challenge of Islam. But before doing that, I think it is necessary to write a few words of intramural discussion within the Christian community of faith about challenges to the doctrine of the Trinity that we ourselves confront. I mention them as a way of clearing the ground before we turn to the discussion between Islam and Christianity.

The first one I call skeptical rationalism. This is the idea that sees the Trinity as irreconcilably at odds with the clear light of human reason, that it is actually superstition, that it is numerical nonsense or worse. We often associate this position with views that have arisen since the Enlightenment, and there is no shortage of such philosophers and others who have made this charge against the Christian doctrine of the Trinity. However, it is not really a new charge; it is one that comes within the Christian family itself. We can trace it back at least as early as Abelard in the Middle Ages, who was accused by Bernard of Clairvaux of denying the reality of God because he sought to apply a more rationalist canon of understanding to the Trinity. There are also the antitrinitarian Protestants, certain radical reformers of the sixteenth century, including the Polish Brethren, the Socinians, and many others. So, within the tradition itself are those who look skeptically on the doctrine of the Trinity.

The second challenge that has arisen within the Christian community we might better classify as Protestant liberalism, though some Roman Catholic theologians actually could well fit this category. The idea is that the Trinity is not really that important. Perhaps the prototypical view here would be by Schleiermacher, who at the end of his seven-hundred-page treatise of theology, *On the Christian Faith*, included on the last page a paragraph about the Trinity. It is as though we have to say something about this, but we should not say much. And where we place this ought at best to be a footnote, an appendage to what really matters, which in the case of Schleiermacher was religious consciousness, a sense of absolute dependence upon the religious reality that is God. This view is woven into most of the standard histories of Christian dogma produced by Protestant liberal scholars in the late nineteenth and early twentieth centuries, the most eminent of whom was Adolf von Harnack. In 1899 he published *The Essence of Christianity*, in which he said that the Trinity was a part of the hellenization of the Christian message, a departure from the preaching of Jesus and the Gospels. More recently, Martin Werner put forth this view in *The Formation of Christian Dogma*.

In addition to skeptical rationalism and Protestant liberalism within the Christian tradition, there also is a great deal of skepticism about the reality of the Trinity and the importance of the Trinity from an unexpected quarter—a group I characterize as fundamentalist reductionists. This may be surprising because I do not know of any real fundamentalist who has ever denied the doctrine of the Trinity, but there is some tendency to shunt it to the side. The classical documents of the fundamentalist controversy do not emphasize teaching on the Trinity. The five fundamentals do not list it anywhere. The Trinity just is not there. More recently, when the Evangelical Theological Society was formed in 1947, there was only one doctrinal affirmation required of all members, and that was a subscription to the doctrine of biblical inerrancy. About ten or twelve years ago a number of Jehovah's Witnesses wished to join this society, and they had no problem with affirming biblical inerrancy. Yet, most ETS members seemed rather uncomfortable having Jehovah's Witnesses in this most orthodox of theological societies. So, somewhat as an afterthought, one might say a knee-jerk reaction, ETS added a second article, affirming the Holy Trinity. This is how the Trinity has often functioned within quite conservative evangelical and fundamentalist theologies.

I have mentioned these three concerns not because I want to pursue them here but because I think it is important to recognize that these are issues we cannot avoid in our discussion with Islam. In our encounter with Muslims, we cannot cast aside belief in the Trinity, for to Muslims, the Christian belief in God as one in three seems not only inherently contradictory but also inexcusably derogatory. It constitutes nothing less than a denial of the unity of God, for which the harsh word *kufr*, which means deliberate truth-concealing and lying about God, is not too severe. Hence, we need to revisit the doctrine of the Trinity with this conversation, new for many of us, in our minds and hearts.

There are several places in the Qur'an where the Trinity seems to be explicitly denied. Let me just mention three of them. According to Surah (chap.) 5:73, "Unbelievers are those who say 'God is one of three.' There is but one God. If they do not desist from so saying, those of them that disbelieve shall be sternly punished." Also, 5:116 says: "Then God will say, this is on the last day, the final judgment, 'Jesus, Son of Mary, did you ever say to mankind, worship me and my mother as gods besides God?' 'Glory be to you,' he will answer, 'I could never have claimed what I have no right to. I told them only what you bade me. I said, Serve God, my Lord and your Lord.'"

Finally, from 4:171: "People of the book, do not transgress the bounds of your religion. Speak nothing but the truth about God. Believe in God and His apostles and do not say 'three.' God will not forgive idolatry. He that serves other gods besides God has strayed far indeed."

Muslim polemicists often cite these verses against the Christian doctrine of the Trinity, but some scholars have questioned whether this is really a valid interpretation. Do these verses and others like them oppose a truly Christian concept of God, or do they misconstrue the latter for what is really a heretical caricature of this teaching? To answer this question, we must return to the world in which Muhammad was born and raised. His grandfather had been the curator of the Kaaba in Mecca. Today this cubelike block structure is the focal point of Muslim worship. We often see it portrayed in media sources and stories about Islam. Before Muhammad, however, this famous shrine was the center of polytheistic worship in Arabia. Camel caravans and Bedouin tribes from the desert went there to offer sacrifices and pay homage to the sacred objects and local deities. The Kaaba was a veritable pantheon of such deities, 360 in all, more than enough for every day of their lunar year. We know the names of some of these gods. The pagans of Mecca claimed three of them, *Allāt, Al-'uzzā*, and *Manāt*, to be the "daughters of Allah" (Surah 53:7). The idea that the Almighty God of Creation could cohabit with mortals and produce progeny was anathema to Muhammad. "What? Shall you have sons?" he asks these Meccan polytheists. "Shall you have sons and Allah daughters?"[1] It was the mission of Muhammad to destroy this kind of idolatry root and branch.

Muhammad was born less than two centuries after Augustine died. Christians had clarified and defined the doctrine of the Trinity only after centuries of controversy and debate within the church. In 325 the Council of Nicea declared that the Son was of the same essence as the Father, thus countering the view of Arius, the presbyter of Alexandria, who believed that the Father had created the Son. Three other important church councils clarified the meaning of this teaching: Constantinople in 381, Ephesus in 431, and finally Chalcedon in 451. The council of 451 declared the incarnate Christ to be one person, the Second Person of the Holy Trinity, in two natures: the one nature fully human, the other nature fully divine. These were and are complex notions. Given the ferocity of the debates and the issues at stake, it is not surprising that many Christians did not grasp it all at once. Indeed, some have not yet grasped it!

Tritheism, which makes a trio out of the Trinity, continued to flourish on the margins of Christianity for several centuries. This heretical view sometimes appeared in sophisticated philosophical garb, such as that of John Philoponus. More often, however, tritheism flourished in the more crass and literal versions of popular piety. Apparently, Muhammad had encountered certain quasi-Christians of this latter sort, who taught something like this: God the Father had sexual intercourse with the Virgin Mary, resulting in the conception of Jesus. Where did such a bizarre idea come from? The early church father Epiphanius tells of a fourth-century heretical sect called the Collyridians. Made up mostly of women, they regarded the Virgin Mary as a goddess and sacrificed little round cakes to her, called *collyrides* (= *collyridae*, Lev. 7:12 Vulg.; cf. Jer. 7:18), hence the name. We have no evidence that Muhammad came into contact with this particular group, but it is not hard to see how an exaggerated devotion to Mary, together with common portrayals of the Madonna and child, might have reinforced Muslim misperceptions of the Christian doctrine of the Trinity. We do know that Muhammad had contact with more orthodox Christian believers later in his life; one of the wives he married, after Khadija's death, was a Coptic Christian from Egypt. However, what is rejected in the Qur'an itself is not the proper Christian doctrine of the Trinity, but rather a heretical belief in three gods. Christians believe just as strongly as Muslims in the oneness of God. We can only agree with the Qur'an in its rejection of a concocted tritheism.

As we all know, the word "Trinity" is not found in the Bible, and this has produced a great deal of consternation among, particularly again, radical Protestant and fundamentalist Christians who want to base their belief and even their language, insofar as possible, on the exact words of the Holy Scriptures. And yet the Bible itself is thoroughly trinitarian from beginning to end. Despite the fact that Islam regards the Bible as corrupted and unreliable, the Qur'an itself encouraged Muslims to read the Law, the Prophets, the Psalms, and the Gospels. It thus is imperative for Christians to understand the biblical basis of the trinitarian doctrine of God. In simplest terms we can say this: The doctrine of the Trinity is the necessary theological framework for understanding the story of Jesus as the story of God; or put otherwise, it is the exposition of the Old Testament affirmation "God is one," and the New Testament confession "Jesus is Lord," neither of which can be understood apart from the person of the Holy Spirit (Deut. 6:4; 1 Cor. 12:3).

It would take another essay, and I think it would be an important one, to talk about how we proceed from these basic biblical affirmations—"God is one," "Jesus is Lord," "The Holy Spirit is a personal reality"—to the language of Nicea, Chalcedon, and so forth. We must presuppose some development of doctrine. This is not a bad idea for evangelicals or for Protestants in general to entertain. We should not imagine that when the disciples of the imprisoned John come to Jesus, they say, "Tell us who you really are." Instead, John wants to know to whom he has been pointing others. Jesus does not say to the disciples of John, "Go back and tell your master, I am God of God, Light of Light, very God of very God, begotten not made" (cf. Matt. 11:2–6; Luke 7:19–23). This is not the language of the Gospels, so it is incumbent upon us to talk about how we move from that biblical language about the reality of God to the confessional language of the early councils and creeds. It was the view of Harnack, Martin Werner, and many others that this was a devolution, a bad move, away from the primal realities, the focus upon "the fatherhood of God and the brotherhood of man," as it was called in the late nineteenth century. I maintain that all the Protestant, Catholic, and Orthodox believers who stand within the great tradition of Christian faith have to reject that reductionistic interpretation.

Now I want to look at the three basic affirmations of Scripture with which we must begin. God is one, Jesus is Lord, and the Holy Spirit is personal. We must begin with the confession "God is one." Christians are just as vehement as Jews and Muslims in affirming what is known in Islam as *tawhid*: loyally recognizing the fundamental unity of God, a sentiment enshrined in the first formula of the *Shahada*: "There is no God but God." Whenever a Muslim baby is born, the mother or nursemaid who brings it into this world takes the infant into her arms, puts breath into its face, and repeats this testimony: "There is no God but God, and Muhammad is the prophet of God." To confess the *Shahada* in the presence of two of more witnesses and to mean it sincerely is what it means to become a Muslim. If any of you wish to convert to Islam, you will be required to do this: to make this confessional statement, "There is no God but God, and Muhammad is the prophet [or, the messenger] of God." Nevertheless, this confession—at least the first part of it, "There is no God but God"—goes back to the *Shema*: "Hear, O Israel: the Lord our God, the Lord is one" (Deut. 6:4 NIV). This thought is repeated not only in the Old Testament but also in the New Testament. Jesus himself quotes it in Mark 12:29, "Hear, O Israel, the Lord our God, the Lord is one. Love the Lord your God with all your heart and with all your soul and with all your mind and with all your strength" (NIV). Jesus believed and taught the oneness of God as foundational to his own messianic vocation (cf. Paul in 1 Cor. 8:6).

How did this belief in the oneness of God arise within the faith of Israel? It was the cornerstone of God's self-revelation to Moses and the prophets over against the polytheism of the culture around them. Like Arabia in the time of Muhammad, the ancient world of the Jews was filled with numerous competing deities. It was a world in which people regarded natural elements—animals, rivers, trees—as divine or at least under the control of various divinities. Out of this setting arose the tradition of idolatry, against which the Old Testament prophets blasted again and again with furious power. Polytheism is the religion of paganism. The Hebrew prophets attacked it as vigorously and sometimes as violently as Muhammad did in Mecca. Why? In the worship of the idols they saw a relapse into the world of unreality. This is why Jeremiah scorned the idols of wood and silver made by the craftsmen who painted and covered them in purple and blue clothes: all dressed up but nowhere to go. "There they are," he mocks, "senseless, foolish, worthless frauds, the objects of mockery. They cannot speak or walk but must be carried about everywhere like the dummies they really are, like a scarecrow in a melon patch" (cf. Jer. 10). By contrast, the God who created heaven and earth is the living God, the eternal King, the maker of all things; he alone is worthy of worship and praise.

The writers of the biblical books do not arrive at the nature and character of God by philosophical speculation but by looking at the words and acts of God in history. Nothing is more evident in the Old Testament than the fundamental oneness of God. Yet, in the context of such an unyielding monotheism, we can already in the Old Testament recognize foreshadowings of the trinitarian revelation. The Old Testament reveals the unity of God to us as a differentiated oneness, and church fathers referred to the evidences of this as *vestigia trinitatis*.

Now I turn to that second affirmation, "Jesus is Lord." The Old Testament reveals the unity of God, and the New Testament reiterates and confirms it. The gospel gives that unity a fuller, deeper exposition in the light of Jesus's life and ministry. The Old Testament affirmation "God is one" is matched by the New Testament confession "Jesus is Lord." To call Jesus Lord, not just with the lips but also from the heart, is to become a Christian. Perhaps here you see a parallel to the *Shahada* in Islam. And calling Jesus Lord, not only with the lips but also from the heart, can only happen through the power of the Holy Spirit, as Galatians 4:6 and 1 Corinthians 12:3 tell us. In the New Testament, saying

"Jesus is Lord" is a way of declaring the deity of Jesus Christ, of affirming his essential oneness with the Father.

More clearly than anywhere else, this reality confronts us in the Gospel of John, and particularly in that opening prologue: "In the beginning was the Word, and the Word was with God, and the Word was God." Three books in the Bible begin roughly the same way, with that expression "In the beginning." There is 1 John 1:1: "That which was from the beginning, which we have heard, which we have seen with our eyes, which we have looked upon, and our hands have handled, of the Word of Life" (KJV). This beginning is obviously a reference to the beginning of Jesus's earthly life and ministry, the incarnation. We are eyewitnesses to this, John says. Also, the first verse in the Bible says: "In the beginning God created the heavens and the earth" (Gen. 1:1 NIV). This beginning is that creative moment when God spoke and worlds, which were not, came into being at the sound of his voice.

The Fourth Evangelist also refers to the beginning: "In the beginning was the Word, and the Word was with God, and the Word was God" (John 1:1). It is a beginning that antedates the incarnation. It goes beyond and even before the creation. It is a beginning before all other beginnings: in Greek, simply *en archē*, that primordial first principle of all things and all time. In the "beginning" that we can recognize only as in "eternity" was "the Word, and the Word was with God, and the Word was God." The Word was *pros ton theon*, with God, face to face with God. John 1:18 tells us that Jesus was at the Father's side. "No one has ever seen God, but God the One and Only, who is at the Father's side, has made him known" (NIV), or literally, "has exegeted him." The translation just quoted, "The One . . . who is at the Father's side," is weak and inadequate. Here the King James Version comes much closer to capturing something of the reality of the New Testament language. "In the bosom of the Father" is so much better than "at the Father's side." Having someone "at your side" is language we use quite loosely. Suppose you are going to the ball game, and your chum is with you and walking by your side. This is not the concept here in John 1:18. Being "in the bosom of the Father" expresses a kind of intimacy and mutuality that goes far beyond this contemporary language of being at someone's side (cf. John 13:23 KJV, Jesus reclining at table next to the beloved disciple).

The one verse in John's prologue that summarizes the Christian faith more completely than perhaps any other text in the New Testament is John 1:14: "And the Word was made flesh, and dwelt among us, (and we beheld his glory, the glory as of the only begotten of the Father,) full of grace and truth" (KJV). Again, I am quoting the King James rendering. Some modern versions read: "And the Word became a human being," but again, that translation does not say enough. The original meaning goes deeper, stronger than that. "The Word became flesh" (NIV/NRSV). Flesh is the part of our human reality that is most vulnerable. It becomes sick, it grows tired, it experiences disease, decay, and death. This is the stupendous claim the Bible makes: that God was in Christ, reconciling the world unto himself (2 Cor. 5:19); that the Word who was in the beginning with God and was God, face to face with God and in the very bosom of the Father, this one and not another became flesh and dwelt among us (John 1:1, 14, 18).

Now we come to the third affirmation: The Holy Spirit is a personal reality. The very fact that from inspired Holy Writ we add the adjective "Holy" to Spirit implies personality. It is possible to talk about the numinous. One can converse about Rudolf Otto's idea of the transcendent numinous power that fascinates us, all without bringing personality into the concept. Indeed, much spirit language in contemporary theology, I think, veers toward the impersonal. However, once we introduce "Holy" Spirit we are, ipso facto, talking about a personal reality, and in the New Testament the Holy Spirit does things that only a person can do. The Holy Spirit baptizes us (1 Cor. 12:13). The Holy Spirit grieves and can be grieved (Eph. 4:30). The Holy Spirit groans as we groan in prayer (Rom. 8:23, 26). These are things that only a person can do. So, we find these three core affirmations in the New Testament: God is one, Jesus is Lord, and the Holy Spirit is personal.

Now I want to step back for a moment and ask, "What does all this mean in terms of our trinitarian affirmation vis-à-vis Islam?" I ask this in terms of two provocative issues: (1) Is monotheism enough? Is it enough to be monotheistic? (2) Does God need a Son? Why does he need a Son?

Let us tackle the first question: Is monotheism enough? The word "Allah" is found 2,685 times in the Qur'an. Muhammad did not invent this word. Today in the Christian apologetic against Islam, a certain strain of thought claims that Allah is the name of a foreign deity, an idol, the moon god. In fact, Allah was a common word of address for God used by Arabic Christians centuries before Muhammad was born. Today, still, millions of Arabic-speaking Christians all over the world address God as Allah. Whoever reads an Arabic New Testament finds this word "Allah" for God. In Malaysia in the last few years, Muslim authorities have actually ordered Arabic-speaking Christians *not* to refer to God as Allah lest the Christian Allah be confused in the popular mind with the Allah of Islam. This controversial policy ignores the historical fact that Christians called God Allah long before Muslims did; it also ignores the Qur'anic affirmation that Christians and Muslims have the same God. This scene reminds us of the confusion that arises when we ignore either the convergence or the contrast between differing conceptions of the one God whom both Islam and Christianity professionally and passionately claim.

The term "Allah" is the contraction of two Arabic words, *il* and *ilah*, "the god." People commonly used the word "Allah" in pre-Islamic Arabia, sometimes associated with an individual's personal name. We know that it is a name, for example, of those who were in the family of Muhammad, those who cared for the Kaaba in Mecca. When Christians read the Qur'an, they are often struck by how similar the Qur'anic depiction of God sounds to that which we find in the Bible. For example, the closing verses of Surah 59 describe Allah as omniscient, compassionate, and merciful. He is God besides whom there is no other. He is the sovereign Lord, the holy one, the giver of peace, the keeper of faith, the guardian, the mighty one, the all-powerful, the most high, the God exalted above all idols, the creator, the originator. Islam remembers ninety-nine beautiful names for God, all of which, rightly understood, Christians also would want to affirm and indeed did affirm long before they were found to be written in the Qur'an. Again and again the Qur'an portrays God as majestic, glorious, almighty, all-wise, and supreme in every way. As Christians who speak with a sense of accountability to the biblical revelation, we can object to nothing with regard to these names.

So, how are we to explain the overlapping content between the God of Muhammad and the God who reveals himself in the

Bible? If we do not believe, as Christians do not, that the Qur'an is a literal transcript of an infallible book conveyed to Muhammad by the angel Gabriel, there are at least two other ways of accounting for the fact that Islam does teach many true and important things about God. First of all, Abraham may have passed on to Ishmael and his descendents after him the special revelation God had given him, including a monotheistic belief in a creator God whom humans must worship. Indeed, we encounter other monotheisms in Arabia and that part of the world before the time of Muhammad. No less than an evangelical theologian, Carl F. H. Henry, has suggested that this primordial revelation might be a source of some of the monotheistic strivings that we find in early Islam. Even apart from channels of special revelation, it is evident from Scripture that fallen human beings can and do know many true things about God on the basis of his general revelation, in both the conscience within and the cosmos without. This natural knowledge of God has been shattered, as Calvin says in the *Institutes*, but not completely effaced by the effects of the fall. So, on the basis of God's general revelation, there is this primordial awareness that God is and that, indeed, God is one.

Paul's encounter with the religious leaders of Athens on Mars Hill has much to teach us about our approach to persons of other faiths (Acts 17:22–34). In the account of Paul's visit to Athens, we find a model of interreligious dialogue and Christian witness at the same time. Unlike certain religious pluralists today, Paul did not assume that all the various forms of religious devotion he observed were equally valid pathways to the same God. The flea market of idols he encountered in Athens greatly distressed him. When he preached about Jesus and the resurrection, some of his hearers thought he was proposing the addition of two new deities to the already overcrowded pantheon of Athens. This led Paul into a dialogue about the nature of the true God in whom he believed, the God who raised Jesus from the dead.

Significantly, though, Paul did not begin his discourse by bashing the false gods of the Athenians, though elsewhere his preaching did lead to iconoclastic riots (as in Acts 19). Instead, he began by identifying what was missing in the religious worldview of his conversation partners. The fact that the Athenians had built an altar "to an unknown god" indicated that there was a real, if unrecognized, sense of inadequacy that Paul could address with the positive content of the Christian gospel. He did this by pointing to precisely the two places where God has made himself known to every person of every religious tradition: the created order and the human conscience. Paul showed great sensitivity in quoting, not the inspired Old Testament as he always did when speaking to the Jews, but pagan poets familiar to the Greeks. He certainly did not give a stamp of approval to everything these poets had said, but in their writings he found some true statements that confirmed what the Bible teaches about human beings and their relationship to God. Paul did not hesitate to use these non-Christian sources in his evangelistic appeal, but neither did he stop with this acknowledgement of common ground. He went on to tell them who Jesus was in relation to the God of creation. Paul preached Jesus Christ crucified, risen, and coming again. He pointed toward the day of judgment and called for a decision. Finally, Paul called on his listeners to repent and believe the gospel; according to Acts 17:34, several responded positively to his appeal and became followers of Jesus.

Most orthodox Muslims would have no problem with much of Paul's sermon on Mars Hill. God is the creator and sovereign Lord of history. He is transcendent and immanent. There will be a final judgment. However, the point about God raising Jesus from the dead introduces a deep divergence that cannot be explained away as a mere historical dispute about what happened on Good Friday or Easter Sunday. This difference also has important implications for how we understand the reality of God himself. Christianity and Islam cannot simply embrace one another as sister religions on the basis of a shared monotheism without regard to questions about Jesus and his cross and resurrection.

So, is monotheism enough? Suppose we assume that the God of the Bible and Allah in Islam are not two separate gods, but the same God differently understood, as many Muslims who have become Christians explain their own conversion to Christ. If so, then we have to go on to ask the further question: Is the Father of Jesus the God of Muhammad? We can find help from Kenneth Cragg, the great missionary to the Middle East and an Islamist, now in his nineties and still living in Oxford. He helps sort out this difficulty by recognizing that Muslims and Christians speak of the same subject when they speak of God, but they use widely differing predicates in what they say about him.[2] As we have seen, Christians and Muslims do share in common a number of predicates about God, the ninety-nine beautiful names, for example. Christians, though, predicate something essential and irreversible about God that no Muslim can accept: we call him our heavenly Father.

This leads me to my second provocative question: Does God need a Son? Around the side of the beautiful Dome of the Rock in Jerusalem, written in Arabic, are the words "God has no son," a direct quotation from the Qur'an. Since it faces the Church of the Holy Sepulcher, across the blood-stained pavement of the ancient city of Jerusalem, no other expression could so pointedly illuminate the one fundamental difference between Christianity and Islam. One building says that God has no son; the other, the Church of the Holy Sepulcher, proclaims that here, according to ancient Christian tradition, God the Son suffered, died, and rose again.

Most Christians, when they think about the Trinity at all, only think about it in terms of how it affects them, and this is understandable. What does the Trinity have to do with our coming to faith? Theologians refer to this understanding as the economic Trinity. The Father sends the Son into the world, the Son of God bears our sins on the cross, the Holy Spirit gives us new life in Jesus Christ. This economic way of speaking about the Trinity shows how God works outside of himself in order to accomplish his purposes in creation and redemption, how he fulfills his will in history and providence.

It is a good thing that we focus our attention here, certainly, but there is another aspect to the reality of the Trinity that theologians call, somewhat officiously perhaps, the ontological Trinity or the immanent Trinity. That refers to who God is within himself, and here we must proceed with great caution. During the Reformation, Philipp Melanchthon put the caution this way: "We do better to adore the mysteries of deity than to investigate them."[3] Yes, but what if what God does is unrelated to who he is? Can we really trust him? In John 17:3 the economic Trinity and the ontological Trinity are brought together in a single verse: "Now this is eternal life: that they may know you, the only true God, and Jesus Christ, whom you have sent" (NIV). The Father who wills to be known, and the Christ who has been sent to make him known—the two belong inseparably together. This is why Jesus can say with such boldness what no other religious leader has ever dared to claim: "Anyone who has seen me has seen the Father" (John 14:9 NIV).

In seeking to understand the relationship of Jesus Christ to the Father who had sent him, the early church faced two christological dangers. These two dangers precipitated a crisis in the doctrine of the Trinity. The first was modalism, a view claiming that the Trinity is three different modes or masks God wears at different times in salvation history. In the Old Testament he appears as the Father, in the New Testament as the Son, and now, in the age of the church, we experience God as the Holy Spirit. Not only does this view contradict the witness of Scripture—for example, Jesus prays to the Father while on earth—but it also eliminates the possibility of relationality within the divine being of God himself. How could the Father send the Son if there were no distinction between them? How does the Holy Spirit proceed from the Father—or in the Western understanding, from both the Father and the Son—if there is no distinction to be made? If modalism eliminates self-distinction within God, then subordinationism, of the radical kind, undercuts the unity of God. Here the Son and the Spirit are agents of the Father but do not share his essential oneness. Arius taught the most extreme form of subordinationism, claiming that the Son was a creature made by God, an exalted creature to be sure, greater than any other creature, yes, but nonetheless a creature.

The tension between these two poles of christological thinking led to the crisis of the Council of Nicea in 325. Athanasius served as the bishop of Alexandria in Egypt. Arius was a presbyter in his church. The conflict became so intense that the emperor (Constantine I) summoned all the bishops in the Christian world to gather at Nicea in 325 and resolve this dispute. There they formulated a creed, which with a few later changes Christian churches all over the world still recite. On the crucial point of contention between Arius and Athanasius, the Nicene Creed says: "We believe . . . in one Lord Jesus Christ, the only-begotten Son of God, begotten of his Father before all the worlds, God of God, Light of Light, very God of very God, begotten, not made, being of one substance with the Father." One of the prime arguments against Arius's view was that it left the church with a Christ who was not worthy for believers to worship. If Jesus was less than fully divine, it would be idolatrous to worship him, according to the Hebrew Scripture: "You shall have no other gods before me" (Exod. 20:3). This is precisely the point Muslims also make, that people are to worship none other than God. Thus, *kufr* is that horrible unforgivable sin of associating something with God that is not God. Muslims would be exactly right in pressing this charge against Christians if Jesus indeed were anything less than wholly divine.

Athanasius made the further point that if Jesus was not *homoousios* (of the same substance) with the Father, he could not be "the Savior of the world" (John 4:42). Arius had ridiculed the idea that God could beget a Son. After all, everyone knows that God is above all aspects of carnal procreation and that he does not reproduce sexually, just as Islam teaches. God is one, the eternal God; he begat none, nor was he begotten; none is equal to him. Athanasius and the theologians in the Nicene tradition who followed him, especially the Cappadocians, sought to explain the begottenness of the Son in a way that avoided both the sterility of Arius's God and the crass literalism derived from Greek mythology. The Nicene formula described the Son as both the same in substance with the Father and yet in some way also distinct from the Father. He was God of God (or, *from* God), Light *from* Light, very God *from* very God. So the challenge was to explain this fromness without violating the sameness. They did this by declaring that the Son was begotten, but not begotten in the way that human fathers beget or generate their earthly children. No, the Son of the heavenly Father was begotten from all eternity (cf. Prov. 8:22–31). He did not come to be at a point in time. There never was a time when he was not. From eternity the Father and the Son have always existed in the relationship of total and mutual self-giving. This kind of eternal begetting would clearly not be possible if the Father were selfish with his glory, power, or majesty. Nevertheless, this image of a selfish, ungenerous God is at the root of contemporary atheism today.

The image that comes to my mind is that of a character in George Eliot's novel *Silas Marner*.[4] Silas Marner was a miser. He was actually a wealthy man, with a lot of money, but nobody knew it. Silas appeared to be stingy, poor, and narcissistic. He kept all of his money under his bed, in a chest filled with gold coins. Every night he would pull out this chest of coins, take out the coins, stroke them, admire them, count them, and then put them back again, never spending a penny. Many people think God is like Silas Marner, the miser. He possesses all of this glory, all of this power, all of this wonderful reality—but he keeps it to himself. He hoards it. However, this is not the God we confess in the Nicene faith. This God, the God Athanasius and the Cappadocian fathers proclaimed, is a God who is unspeakably generous. He gives all that he has to the Son in an eternal interchange of holy love. Neither is the Son self-seeking, for love seeks not its own (cf. 1 Cor. 13:5 KJV); instead, he returns all that he has received to the glory of the Father, with the Holy Spirit as the bond of unity between the two, as Augustine would show in *De Trinitate*. The mystery of God's unity is thus a unity of love. When we peer into the heart of God, we find not solitary absoluteness, the alone with the alone, which is Arius's term for God, but the mystery of eternal love and relationship: a begetting without a beginning, and an indwelling without an ending.

How do we know this? Not by looking from a distance at God's majestic power and his faithful governance of the universe. Nor, indeed, by reflecting on the awareness we have of God within our conscience. General revelation can tell us, as Thomas Aquinas would teach us and show us, that there is a God but not who this God is. Only from God's self-revelation in the history of Israel and in the event of Jesus Christ do we learn the nature of the unknown God whom people seek after and hint at in many religions and cultures of the world. Athanasius pointed to a number of texts in John's Gospel where this mutual self-giving between the Father and the Son is explicitly stated. John 3:35 tells us that the Father loves the Son and has placed everything in his hands. Or again, "As the Father has life in himself, so he has granted the Son to have life in himself" (5:26 NIV). For his part, the Son does not seek his own will, but the will of the Father who sent him. He does nothing on his own authority, but declares what the Father has taught him (8:28). Because this is true, Jesus can make those remarkable statements that he and the Father are one, and that knowing Jesus issues in knowing the Father as well. This is why Jesus can say that when people believe in him, they believe not just in him, but also in the one who sent him

(12:44). In the famous text of 14:1, Jesus says, "You believe in God, you believe also in me" (author's translation). Here we can read the Greek verbs in either the indicative mood (as above) or the imperative: "Believe in God, believe also in me." Hence, Jesus leaves us with this meaning: What we see in the life and ministry of Jesus, including his being delivered up by the Father to the death of the cross, is not an aberration. It is not an accident. It is the revelation of who God really is: the one the New Testament calls the God and Father of our Lord Jesus Christ.

Bare monotheism divorced from the rich content of biblical faith is not enough. Or again, as Bishop Kenneth Cragg has so aptly put it, bare monotheism is ultimately barren.[5] The doctrine of the Trinity is not peripheral; it is essential to our understanding of the character and nature of the one true God. And here are five implications of this foundational Christian truth.

1. *God is one but not alone.* The doctrine of the Trinity does not destroy the unity of God but reinforces it. It defines that unity in terms of a fecundity and a richness, a texturedness, so to speak, within the reality of the one who is the Father, the Son, and the Holy Spirit.

2. *God is love.* In the biblical view, relationship is constitutive for God himself. The Father gives, the Son receives, the Holy Spirit proceeds. God is love. Here is not simply the fact that God loves us, though that is a wonderful thing; yes, John 3:16 is true, but the Bible says more than that. It says that God does not love us because Jesus died for us, but Jesus died for us because God loves us. God is love.

3. *God is free to be gracious.* The rich theological heritage of the Reformed tradition—stemming from Augustine, including Calvin, and leading to Karl Barth—emphasizes this very important point. God's decision to create and redeem the world was not motivated by any external constraint, nor by any compulsion to make up for any deficit in his own being. God is the one who wills to love in freedom. God is free to be gracious.

4. *God is personal.* The doctrine of the Trinity tells us that relationality, that personality, is at the heart of the universe. Thomas Hardy once referred to God as "the dreaming, dark, dumb Thing that turns the handle of this idle show."[6] Again, we are back to the Silas Marner type of stingy God, hoarding the glory to himself, keeping the show running but not getting very

involved in it: the God of Deism. Thomas Hardy's God is devoid of relationship. It is stark, speechless, obscure, remote, a hideous caricature of the real God. This is why the true alternative to Christian trinitarian theology today is not competing monotheisms such as Islam or something else, but atheism.

5. *God is sufficiently sovereign to come as well as to send.* Here, perhaps, the contrast with Islam comes full circle. For in Islam revelation is, essentially, what God's project is about, what Allah's project is about, in this world and in our history. God reveals himself through prophets, beginning with Adam and culminating with Muhammad through the Qur'an. It is a revelation. What is missing here is a concept of redemption. God is not only a revealer; God is a redeemer as well. The trinitarian understanding of God tells us that this God is sufficiently sovereign to come as well as to send.

In the early church, the Gnostics asked, "What did God do? Did he bring anything new in sending his Son?" To which the early church replied that he brought everything new in sending his Son because he brought himself. One of my former teachers, Arthur C. McGill, expressed it so well: "God's divinity does not consist in his ability to push things around, to make and break, to impose his will from the security of some heavenly remoteness, to sit in grandeur while all the world does his bidding. Far from staying above the world, he sends his own glory into it. Far from imposing, he invites and persuades. Far from demanding service from men in order to enhance himself, he gives his life in service to men for their enhancement."[7] God acts toward the world in this way because within himself this is how he is: a life of eternal self-giving.

8

The Soteriological Importance of the Divine Perfections

Ellen T. Charry

Western Christian theology is undergoing a great upheaval about how to speak of God. Beginning with Adolf von Harnack with an explosion of concern in the 1980s and 1990s, scholars have raised an ecumenical cry to reject traditional talk of God in terms of being and to speak instead of God as acts, relationships, or the event of relationship in order to highlight the work of God in "his" three distinctions, self-realizations, instances, identities, or personae. Christian theology has always spoken of events or acts that God accomplishes or relationships that God has, but such talk has generally assumed that events accomplished by God and relationships taking place within or with God presuppose a nature, essence, or substance performing or having them. The current revolution in thought opposes this notion of a divine nature apart from or prior to the acts or relations of God.

Thomas Aquinas established the academic convention of talking first of a divine essence with his presentation of the doctrine of God in the *Summa theologica*. This work begins with the treatises "The Divine Unity" and "The Divine Persons." It is only in the last question (qu. 43) of the latter treatise that he discusses the missions, or sendings, of the three divine self-realizations as testified in Scripture. Thus, standard scholastic procedure was to discuss first the divine nature or being, defined as perfections, then the relations among the instances of God (beyond time-space), and finally the missions of the instances in the world (time-space). This three-stage order seems to imply that the processions and the missions derive from the divine being/nature/substance, which is composed of eternal perfections—the divine DNA, so to speak, that characterizes God. The assumption here seems to be that a thing must be before it can do, an idea that is, on the face of it, quite reasonable. The philosophical problem is that the perfections that constitute the divine nature are not "things" but notions or forms: goodness, beauty, wisdom, and so on. The open question is whether these "exist."

The current revolution takes strong exception not only to scholastic procedure but also to the ontological presupposition that being precedes doing as not only badly outmoded but flat-out wrong, not because it presents God badly but because it forwards a wrong vision of reality altogether.[1] Reality happens in time-space, not in a set of ideas. Therefore, instead of defining God as a clump of perfections, we should define God as action(s) or relationship because only things that happen in time-space exist; ideas do not. The assumption now is that doing *is* being—to act is to be—and there is nothing behind doing/acting. We are what we do, so to speak, or at least God is what he does. It is and always was misleading to begin a presentation on reality or God with a discussion of the divine perfections (as Thomas does) as constituting the divine nature because—contrary to Plato and his followers—there is no being or nature, no "DNA" of anything apart from or behind instances of it, that is, behind God's doings. Thus it would be clearer to begin talking about God either with the processions of the three divine self-realizations as they relate to one another or with, preferably, their missions in history as witnessed to in Scripture and presumably in everything else comparably. On the theological side, the new trinitarianism, offered in various forms by Catholics, Protestants, and Eastern Orthodox alike, is now, as Karen Kilby aptly says, "the new orthodoxy."[2]

Examining the Complaint

To my knowledge, the first writer to object to the classical formulation of the doctrine of God was the great historian of doctrine Adolf von Harnack. He complained that the classical Christian doctrine of God subordinated the living God of Sinai to a collection of philosophical abstractions that render God impersonal, and he blamed the problem—wrongly, in my judgment—on Augustine of Hippo. He correctly noted that Augustine's treatment of the Trinity succeeded in destroying the last remains of pre-Nicene economic trinitarianism, associated with Justin Martyr, Irenaeus, and Tertullian, which interpreted God in terms of God's activities, on behalf of the Nicene insistence that all instances of God are alike the one same God. "This speculation, which attempts to construe the most immanent of immanent Trinities and to sublimate the Trinity into a unity, just because it does this, discards everything in the way of a basis in historical religion and loses itself in the paradoxical distinctions and speculations, while at the same time it is not able to give clear expression of its new and valuable thought. The great work of Augustine, 'De Trinitate,' can scarcely be said to have promoted piety anywhere or at any time."[3] Harnack's objection is that with Augustine the distinctiveness of the Son and the Spirit resolves back into the one God and thereby the specificity of the work of God is lost.

The fourth-century Arian controversy pressed Nicene theologians to demonstrate that Christ and the Spirit are not lesser gods or creatures but truly God himself, so that the work that they do to rescue us from corruption and decay is truly the work of God. Athanasius of Alexandria did the spadework with the word *homoousios*, and Augustine concluded or consolidated Athanasius's work in his great masterpiece De Trinitate (*The Trinity*). Harnack's charge is that Augustine overcorrected Arianism with the principle of appropriation, or, more aptly, attribution, spelled out in the so-called Athanasian Creed (although it is post-Augustine), according to which all three instances of God are equally God—so that each instance is essentially the same as each other even though specific actions are attributed to or appropriate to only one—and equally participate in each and every divine activity. The thrust of the criticism is that this teaching is insufficiently trinitarian and overly monotheistic because the three divine distinctions are not ultimate. If each is exactly what the others are except for designation, their common "substance," not the actions that they perform in history, saves us. The actions of God point beyond themselves to Godness itself, and that is the perfections. The complaint is that this renders the missions instrumental to the perfections and these do not exist apart from instances. In short, the complaint is that the classical doctrine is incoherent.

Although the complaint is now urgently pressed, it could not have arisen before aspersions were cast on the transcendent realm by David Hume and especially Immanuel Kant, who taught moderns that even if the transcendent realm where God is is real, we cannot know it. Knowledge is restricted to what we know through our senses. This limits our knowledge to historical events. At this point, talk of the divine being as perfections becomes impossible. This accounts for the current urge to finally rid the Christian tradition of these lifeless abstractions, which subvert the living God active and present with and for us at Sinai and beyond.

Augustine did not have such epistemic anxieties, not because the transcendentals were for him forms to be admired from afar—as perhaps they were for Plato—but because the incarnation had enabled us to know them through divine action in history. He discusses the perfections themselves only at the end of *De Trinitate* (15.2), although all along he has kept them in view as they are disclosed by the missions. Note the direction here from material to immaterial; it is the same direction as that taken by Karl Barth in the twentieth century.[4] Unfortunately, Augustine's procedure has rarely been noted in criticisms of the classical doctrine, which often run together the fact that we know the perfections with the way in which we know them.

Although it is undeniable that Augustine turned to the Greek heritage for assistance in articulating the doctrine of God, his interest comes, in my judgment, from moral and psychological concerns. He wanted us to benefit from God's beauty and to satisfy our moral cravings. Unless we can see and name the virtues to emulate and the vices to shun, how can we envision a better life for ourselves? If we can discern both wisdom and folly in our neighbors through the biblical stories and perhaps even in the natural world, are we not entitled to believe analogously that in longing for and attempting to cultivate wisdom in ourselves following those invitations, we are approaching the divine beauty itself? But here we are getting ahead of ourselves.

To return to the modern history that drives the complaint after Hume and Kant: moving from the phenomenal to the noumenal will supposedly not work. According to this view, modernity seems to be stuck with a God defined by perfections that we cannot know because they are presented as abstractions and not as realizations. Thus the current objection to the traditional positing of the divine being—the ontological issue—is motivated by an epistemological question: can we know God? The trinitarian revolutionaries hone in on this point by privileging the scriptural witness over the wisdom-seeking traditions. We can know the God of the fathers but not the god of the lovers of wisdom. Augustine, too, worked from the scriptural text, but he did not find it incompatible with Greek wisdom as moderns tend to.

Every revolution pays a price for the advances it portends, and the current one is no exception. Here the price is the spiritual and soteriological value of the divine attributes or perfections. The danger is not so much that they will be subordinated to the processions or the missions. Indeed, such subordination may help the problem identified, methodologically speaking. A problem would arise, however, if the soteriological value of the divine attributes or perfections is no longer recognized at all. An impetus for the current revolution in thought is broad agreement that the divine nature, or "Godness," specified by perfections, has no spiritual utility and no intellectual credibility because, in scholastic presentations, they floated in midair, attached to and grounding nothing existing. The attributes pack no soteriological punch but are lifeless essences, vacant ideas inherited from classical culture that dangle helplessly in front of moderns who inhabit a different world made up of time, not being in general. The intent of this revolution is not to deny the divine being but to relocate and redefine it in and as specific actions and relations. That is, the doctrinal revolutionaries argue that the divine self-realizations—Father, Son, and Holy Spirit—do not derive from or depend upon the divine perfections or attributes, some substrate beyond anything in the scriptural witness, but rather the reverse: the divine being, including the attributes, depends upon and derives its meaning from the actions and/or relations of the divine self-realizations that should be seen to constitute God as such.

The argument here will be that although, as the revolutionaries note, discussion of the divine perfections apart from the realizations of God—as if they are logically or temporally prior to them—is problematic, this does not mean that the perfections have no soteriological power in themselves. In fact, reversing the received order of discussion from perfections, processions, missions to missions, processions, and only then perfections may indeed help us see the soteriological importance of the divine attributes.

To accomplish this, I make two suggestions: first, that we separate the procedural complaint from the theological complaint and, second, that we realize that, for Augustine, salvation happens in us, not in an action of God. If we follow these suggestions, we can more effectively deal with the problems at hand without neglecting or disparaging the soteriological significance of the divine perfections.

Separating the Issues

One step toward addressing the complaint is to separate the procedural objection to the presentation of the doctrine of God from the theological objection to salvation through the divine perfections. The confusion comes from reading Augustine through Thomas Aquinas, or at least considering Augustine's supposed modalism in his *De Trinitate* and Thomas's presentation of the doctrine of God in his *Summa theologica* (I, qu. 1, arts. 1–16) to be two examples of the same problem: overemphasis on the oneness of God. They are not. Harnack's objection to Augustine is that his insistence that the divine self-realizations are one and the same God falls into philosophical speculation. Others object that this insistence does not adequately stress the divine distinctions. The objection to Thomas is generally similar but concerns specifically the manner of his presentation. Putting the discussion of the divine unity first makes it seem as if the processions and the missions are less important because they are clearly separated from the initial and central concern: the perfections. Failure to distinguish the theological from the procedural concerns makes it difficult to see that we can alter the method in order to view the theological issue more clearly.

The last sentence in the Harnack quotation given above is also noteworthy: "The great work of Augustine, 'De Trinitate,' can scarcely be said to have promoted piety anywhere or at any time." If Augustine's treatment of the Trinity is read through the later Thomistic procedure of setting the discussion of the divine unity before the discussion of the three persons, it is misread because Thomas discussed the perfections apart from any context for understanding them, as if they could stand alone. Harnack thinks that Augustine's teaching is pastorally useless because Harnack read it through Thomas's discussion of divine simplicity and perfection as defining God without reference to the Father, Son, and Holy Spirit. But Augustine never does this. Although he stresses that the three divine self-realizations are one and the same God, Augustine never discusses the perfections as if the perfections were God apart from the Father, Son, and Holy Spirit. The significant objection is that the perfections themselves seem to have no soteriological import. But this is the case only when they are discussed apart from the God disclosed in Scripture, as done by Thomas.

When we separate the theological from the procedural concern, we see that the complaint about the value of the divine perfections does not require discussing them apart from divine activity in history. Then we can see clearly that Augustine did not present the doctrine of God as Thomas did. Augustine was not a scholastic concerned with the divine unity in itself, nor did he engage in philosophical speculation apart from the God of history. Rather, all that he is concerned to show is that the three divine self-realizations discussed in Scripture are equally one and the same God.

Augustine starts with the missions because all our knowledge starts with material things. This indeed is the reason for the incarnation. God comes to us as us because like knows like. We cannot know God as ideas or abstract notions, but—and this speaks to Kant's objection—we can discern values and virtues at work in things that we do know, in this case human life itself. The point is that these values and virtues are, for Augustine as for Thomas, substantive claims about the divine being but, unlike Thomas, Augustine does not discuss them apart from their visibility in one or all of the three divine self-realizations or in us. This point is central for identifying a weakness in the trinitarian revolution.

Locating and Defining Salvation

Having addressed the procedural issue, we turn to the soteriological question of where salvation happens and what it is. The trinitarian revolution is motivated by the desire to locate salvation in the economy. It bolts from Augustine because he locates salvation in the interface between the divine being and the soul to which the economy is instrumental. The two positions differ on not only the location but the content of salvation as well. For Augustine, salvation is spiritual healing and approximation to happiness theologically understood, whereas, for the trinitarian revolutionaries, salvation is assurance of divine favor achieved through the economy. These radically different visions of salvation help explain why Augustine is the archenemy of the radical trinitarian movement and why the new trinitarian vision tends to lose sight of the soteriological value of the divine perfections.

On Augustine's terms, the strange Nicene insistence that a Galilean artisan is God helps us understand the issues because it points to the healing reality that, by knowing God through the three self-realizations, we grow into understanding ourselves better as creatures in this same trinitarian image. We encounter our true identity and thereby come to see God and participate in the divine attributes that we know through these instances. The dogmatic teaching serves this pastoral and soteriological end. Living into the Nicene teaching about the divine persons aids self-knowledge, and true self-knowledge aids a good life, and this is foundational for a strong and healthy society.[5] Augustine's teaching is at once moral, psychological, and social; that is, it is pastoral and spiritual.

By criticizing Augustine's trinitarian theology, Harnack is also attacking the soteriology that it explains, for salvation, according to Augustine, requires our being ferried from the activity in the economy into the divine perfections by means of the classic virtues. Harnack inadvertently raises the question of where salvation is finally located—in an act of God or in internalizing and being conformed to the divine nature to the extent that this is possible for creatures?—and what it is. Augustine argues that salvation takes place in the soul, not in any action of God, and that becoming happy (theologically speaking) is its content. By turning to the text, we can see his position a bit more fully.

The first half of *De Trinitate* (bks. 1–7) exegetes the Nicene teaching scripturally. We understand divine actions described there. Augustine acknowledges that from one perspective, Father, Son, and Holy Spirit operate indivisibly, although various New Testament (but not Old Testament) texts individuate them. For him, which instance of God does which act is significant and decisive for our knowledge, but soteriologically speaking, all acts of God work together to straighten out crooked sinners by bringing them into the beauty and goodness revealed by each of those acts. Augustine explains this teaching of salvation as happiness in book 14: assimilation of that beauty and goodness heals the crooked soul. Finally, it is not immediately the actions of God per se that save us but rather being brought by those acts to know God spiritually so that we love him, and when we love him, our ability to love is transformed. For Augustine, salvation is enabled by God but happens in the soul. The cross is decisive because it lures us into the beauty, wisdom, and goodness of God, in which we partake because we reflect the Trinity itself. Salvation is the slow transformation of the soul into holiness and righteousness as a result of proper self-knowledge and self-love for one who is the image of God. "For now it loves itself with a straight, not a twisted love, now that it loves God; for sharing in him results not merely in its being that image, but in its being made new and fresh and happy after being old and worn and miserable."[6]

Augustine, along with other church fathers, depended on the economy of salvation to ferry us over ourselves and the natural world into the beauty, wisdom, and goodness of God. Here the three divine self-realizations are not ultimate but lead us to the perfections that straighten us out. That is, for Augustine, the economy carries us into the Godhead itself, which is the final agent of the salvation that occurs in us, through the divine attributes that are themselves revealed through the works of the realizations of God sent into the world to carry us into God's goodness and wisdom. The *exitus-reditus* scheme of movement is important here. God enters the world as the Son and the Holy Spirit, who then carry us back to God through their work. The Johannine portrayal of Jesus sent into the world by the Father, doing his work on earth, and returning to the Father deeply influenced Augustine. His longing for God finally was the longing for intimacy with God or for "seeing" him eternally. Included in this longing to see God is the transformation of the self by the attributes that the acts of God disclose. The order of the Augustinian presentation is important. He begins with the missions, which reveal the processions. Through the divine self-realizations, we arrive at the perfections and so God himself in a limited way. Complete rest in that vision is reserved for another day.

The trinitarian revolutionaries object to this soteriology because it locates salvation in the soul of the God-seeker and because it defines salvation as sanctification. For Augustine, salvation is a therapeutic process of psychological and moral transformation that requires taking knowledge about God learned from Scripture and applying it to oneself. Self-transformation is never accomplished without the gift of divine grace, but its possibility lies within our very own trinitarian nature as God created us. That we think triadically provides the foundation for understanding salvation as gradual repair of a distorted, worn-out self that is, theologically speaking, self-hatred. Salvation for Augustine is gradual movement from self-hatred—that is, turning away from God—toward proper self-love, that is, turning toward the source of our true happiness: God. For Augustine, being saved is the long, slow process of becoming happy by seeing, knowing, and loving God.

One objection to this soteriology is that salvation here is what we moderns would call a psychological process. Because it happens in the soul, we must look within to tend to it. This is the argument of the philosophy of mind and moral psychology of *De Trinitate* 8–14. Critics will object that one effect of this theology in the Middle Ages was that Christian piety became inward turning, inviting believers to tend their own garden. Instead of combating self-absorption, as Augustine intended, by turning us from bad self-use toward good self-use and from short-term desire toward God, his theology boomeranged and reinforced self-absorption. Martin Luther is perhaps the paradigmatic example of the problem. He became preoccupied with the status of his salvation. This theology militates against social involvement because we find God through self-examination and so are perhaps saved regardless of commitment to the neighbor. This view is dangerous because, by turning inward, we are likely to become less socially involved and so community life will suffer. In short, the Christian tradition has focused on personal salvation rather than social transformation. Catherine LaCugna, for example, raises this objection. In contrast, she emphasizes that we are saved by the work of God in history, especially through Jesus Christ on the cross, not by self-reflection or, more pointedly, by living into the divine attributes, which bear the taint of Stoic apathia. She prefers action to reflection, of which the ancients were fonder.

I suspect that Augustine would be surprised by the suggestion that his theology is considered antisocial. He would not think that social responsibility and spiritual self-reflection are in tension but mutually dependent. He would respond that social problems are the result of spiritually disordered selves and that the spiritual therapy that he prescribes is the best way to address social dysfunction. Further, his view suggests that only as souls are healed are persons able to use themselves well enough in the world to care for the neighbor well. He does not spell this out, although he often speaks of love of God and neighbor in one breath. Straightening oneself out is requisite for loving others. That is, good self-love and good neighbor-love are of a piece.

Another objection to Augustine's soteriology as developed in *De Trinitate* is that it identifies salvation with sanctification, on the medicinal model. Salvation is becoming a happier and better person in God. This means that the work of the economy of salvation is instrumental to the final end of happiness in the vision of God in the next life. The life and death of Jesus are decisive, according to this view, because they contribute to our understanding of who God is and how God wants us to live. In Augustine's Christology, Christ rescues us from the devil, whom we have followed since the fall; Christ enables us to fall in love with God, from whom we learn better things. This becomes clearest in the Christology of *De Trinitate* 13.13–23, which argues that God chose the crucifixion to free us from the devil in order to teach us always to use power righteously (over ourselves), not to lord it over others. Salvation is not completed but begun by forgiveness of sin through the cross; the reform of the soul is the result of coming to see God's own perfections at work on our behalf and to grow into them. The attentive seeker will see the divine perfections at work in the divine acts and be taken by them. We are not to imitate the crucifixion—God does not relish our suffering—but God, by using power to accomplish justice. The goal here is not imitation of Christ's specific acts. Rather it is our becoming in our own lives wise, just, loving, beautiful, and properly powerful in our own life as God is in his. We can make this connection to God because our mind is triadically structured, so that the powers of the soul work together for this end as the works of the economy display the goodness, justice, and wisdom of the one God.

This soteriology, which finds continuity between God and us, does not sit well with Protestants, for the most part. Protestantism separated justification from sanctification, identifying salvation with the former and considering the latter the appropriate grateful response to justification; salvation happens in the incarnation, not in the soul. It is felt that the older view, put forth here by Augustine, does not provide enough space between God's justifying work and our grateful and passive acceptance of it to satisfy the later craving for humility before divine sovereignty. It attributes too much power to the soul in working out its salvation. Linking knowledge of ourselves to knowledge of God, as Augustine does, is spiritually confusing to us if it suggests that we partake of the divine perfections themselves, even if in a quite limited way. Instead of helping us understand ourselves more deeply as humble recipients of divine mercy, Augustine's treatment of salvation carries us too close to God in our self-understanding and so is in fact spiritually harmful, making us like Icarus, flying too close to the sun. It is ironic that the church father most hated for introducing original sin into the Christian tradition is also criticized for having too positive an understanding of human potential, too high a theological psychology.

As noted, one reason behind the modern contempt for the Augustinian vision of salvation is that the modern view grows out of the medieval stress on humility as the chief Christian virtue whereas Augustine's soteriology is the repair of our ability to love.[7] For Augustine, the repair of love is the key to happiness and empowerment in God; growing into the perfections—especially love—is salvation. Following a quite different soteriology, the radical trinitarian movement locates salvation in the economy, and so it can afford to dispense with a central role for the perfections. But the price paid is the genuine healing of the soul on the Augustinian model.

Retrieving Augustinian Soteriology

As argued above, the concern registered here is not with the rhetorical complaint that pertains to Thomas and those who followed his mode of presentation, for it is well taken and easily corrected. Precisely because we do know empirically, it is probably more helpful, when a scholastic treatment is desired, to inaugurate it with the economy—the missions of the divine self-realizations as testified to by Scripture, as Augustine did beginning with *De Trinitate* 2–3, scouring Scripture for evidence of the Nicene teaching. Since we know sensately best and first, it is best to talk of God in ways that we can grasp. In this the new trinitarians have made a quite helpful suggestion to those who followed Thomas's procedure.

Having noted this point and acknowledged an important contribution of the trinitarian revolutionaries, I direct my concern to the other and more radical suggestion that God be defined by doing rather than being. The discussion often presents the reader with a choice. Either God is act/relation, as with Barth's act-ontology and Zizioulas's relational ontology, or we speak of God as meaningless static essences. This is an understandable response to the problem Kant posed, but it may not be necessary if we grant that Augustinian soteriology considers the perfections not to exist in some pure intellectual space but only in phenomena. Kant's rigid distinction between phenomena and noumena is not the absolute barrier to transcendent knowledge it appears, once we realize that we can see the perfections in the divine actions. Once we do so, we also see that they take up residence in us; they have a life of their own certainly in God but, in Augustine's teaching, also in us.

We have arrived finally at the constructive point of this argument: the reclamation of Augustinian soteriology. Whereas the

trinitarian revolution wants to overthrow Augustinian soteriology, here I have been working to reclaim it on the following
grounds. The missions enable us to see, know, and partake of
God, showing us that our true identity is in him, for we all bear
the trinitarian image even as we think and move in the world.
The divine perfections are soteriologically powerful when viewed
through the divine self-realizations. Then the perfections become
dynamic and transferable. By partaking of them, we are spiritually healed and cease striving against ourselves to our own
self-defeat. The perfections come to abide in us as our ability
to love well improves. Salvation is personal transformation by
growing in wisdom, goodness, justice, and beauty.

In sum, objecting to Augustine's interest in the divine unity is
understandable only when read through Thomas's discussion of
the unity apart from the processions and missions. Once we put
them back into the framework supplied by scriptural testimony,
they spring to life with powerful pastoral and soteriological value.
Augustine was not alone in this view but shared it with his con-
temporaries, as we can see from a brief examination of other
prescholastic theologians: Gregory of Nyssa, Basil the Great,
and Pseudo-Dionysius.

Gregory of Nyssa on the Holy Trinity

Gregory wrote two short treatises defending his doctrine of
God against the charge of tritheism. The lesser-known is "On the
Holy Trinity, and of the Godhead of the Holy Spirit."

> If, on the other hand, we understand that the operation of the
> Father, the Son, and the Holy Spirit is one, differing or varying
> in nothing, the oneness of their nature must needs be inferred
> from the identity of their operation. The Father, the Son, and
> the Holy Spirit alike give sanctification, and life, and light, and
> comfort, and all similar graces. And let no one attribute the power
> of sanctification in an especial sense to the Spirit, when he hears
> the Saviour in the Gospel saying to the Father concerning his
> disciples, "Father, sanctify them in Thy name." So too all the other
> gifts are wrought in those who are worthy alike by the Father, the
> Son, and the Holy Spirit: every grace and power, guidance, life,
> comfort, the change to immortality, the passage to liberty, and
> every other boon that exists, which descends to us.[8]

The point is that the Trinity acts as one in bringing us all the boons of God, no matter which instance of God they come through. A few paragraphs later, Gregory makes the point about the unity of the instances even more strongly, coming quite close to the doctrine of appropriations when he writes that they are not distinguishable by substance but by operations, the distinctions in Scripture being "by appointment."[9] Here the task of the operations is to mediate the gifts of divine goodness, wisdom, beauty, life, light, sanctification, and so on, to us, precisely as is the case with Augustine.[10] We see that at least some aspects of God's character are shared with us, further unifying us with one another in God.

We can become more beautiful, wiser, better, and more righteous, but never utterly. Seeing our salvation come through the divine perfections helps us overcome being nailed to our deeds, so that we grow in goodness as perfections seep into us. They may not be as pastorally useless as some have thought. The most heavily criticized are the perfections of eternality and immutability, for they seem to render God static, inert, and therefore unable to love. Yet, instead of *static*, suppose we used the word *stable*? Stability is the foundation of loyalty and faithfulness. Relying on God's unshakable stability provides security in a fragile and unstable world. This indeed has been, one suspects, the appeal of these absolutes all along. Perhaps they endure because we cannot provide our own stability, centeredness, and integration. Life is too full of missteps and mishaps. Its rapidly changing pace is now enervating. Augustine's most famous sentence sums up their goal: "Our hearts are restless until we find our rest in you."[11] Although such stability as we attribute to God is not possible for us, loyalty and faithfulness are, at least to some degree, and so there is a tiny way in which even the divine stability can become us.

If, as I have suggested, God showers us with the perfections in lesser ways, it may be that strong trinitarian proposals are too strict if they obscure the fact that salvation is the work of the perfections in the soul. We can lose sight of the prescholastic soteriology of participation in the divine perfections if we allow contempt for the matter of presentation of the doctrine to hide the soteriological power of the perfections themselves. Let us hear from another father of the church.

Basil the Great on the Divine Holiness

Basil the Great, who contributed mightily to working out the doctrine of the Trinity, defended the equality and dignity of status of the Holy Spirit with the Father and the Son. He followed Origen in identifying the work of the Spirit with sanctification, as his own soteriological task. Perhaps, unhampered by the *filioque*, Basil sees the Spirit carrying us directly to the vision of God.

> Spirit-bearing souls, illumined by [the Holy Spirit], finally become spiritual themselves, and their grace is sent forth to others. From this comes knowledge of the future, understanding of mysteries, apprehension of hidden things, distribution of wonderful gifts, heavenly citizenship, a place in the choir of angels, endless joy in the presence of God, becoming like God, and, the highest of all desires, becoming God.[12]

The Spirit is the personalized way Christians talk about the holiness of God. The Spirit is appointed to convey that holiness to us, that is, to sanctify us. The recipient of the Spirit's work in the sacraments, for example, is not united with the Spirit only but also with the fullness of God. Salvation happens in the soul's union with divine holiness. To be united with God is to become the perfections in ways appropriate to human nature and life.

A question for the radical trinitarianism of our day is whether, given its distrust of the perfections, it can support this older soteriology of ascent. If salvation takes place in us and not outside or without us, rich discussion of the perfections is essential. Anxiety about the perfections as empty notions seems to miss the point made by the fathers about what it means to know God.

Pseudo-Dionysius and the Divine Names

Let us consider the divine perfections according to another prescholastic theologian, Pseudo-Dionysius. His treatise *De divinis nominibus* (*The Divine Names*) treats the doctrine of God through the myriad names for God in Scripture, including many impersonal names. He begins with a rhapsody on the divine character that he gleans from the texts. The many biblical designations of God themselves name variously the divine simplicity.

In keeping with his language, we might say that divine simplicity gleams with movement and life, where the various characteristics bump up against one another, calling out to us to deepen our grasp of them. He could not have imagined that God's names suggest that God is "impersonal" or static because we use them to describe his beauty, wisdom, and goodness but finally become lost in our own inarticulacy.

The goodness of God is arguably the most basic attribute from Pseudo-Dionysius. Subsequent theologians have contorted themselves to protect it. Pseudo-Dionysius explains it this way:

> The Good returns all things to itself and gathers together whatever may be scattered, for it is the divine Source and unifier of the sum total of things. Each being looks to it as a source, as the agent of cohesion, and as an objective. The Good, as scripture testifies, produced everything and it is the ultimately perfect Cause. In it, "all things hold together" [Col. 1:7] and are maintained and preserved as if in some almighty receptacle. All things are returned to it as their own goal. All things desire it: Everything with mind and reason seeks to know it. Everything sentient yearns to perceive it, everything lacking perception has a living and instinctive longing for it, and everything lifeless and merely existent turns, in its own fashion, for a share of it.[13]

Experience of the goodness of God, then, is immediate and direct, known because God is so named in Scripture. It draws us to itself and "refurbishes and restores the image of God corrupted within [us]." Further, the divine goodness, while "at a total remove from every condition; movement, life, imagination, conjecture, name, discourse, thought, conception, being, rest, dwelling, unity, limit, infinity," is nevertheless "at the center of everything . . . and 'in it all things hold together.'"[14] God's goodness unites all things, even if they cannot understand it. According to Pseudo-Dionysius, the goodness of God is at the center of reality, even if we fail to grasp it on account of our own suffering.

Here there is no anxiety about a stable center of the universe. Granted, the presentation rests on a value system different from that of the contemporary one, which attends to change rather than to stasis whereas those of earlier times preferred rest to struggle. Still, even a perfunctory reading of Pseudo-Dionysius reveals the dynamic quality of his understanding of the goodness of God, which is anything but static, resides in all creation, and draws us to itself so that we might realize our harmony with and within it. For Pseudo-Dionysius, divine simplicity is dynamic, alluring, and illuminating. Further, it provides the sacred canopy that holds all things together. All creatures are bound together in it. In short, a slightly more imaginative treatment of the divine character would reveal not only the dynamism of divine simplicity but also the communion that it establishes with creation.

Once we see divine simplicity teeming with life, we can also see that it is expansive. When the discussion is limited to the traditional traits, others are neglected, and divine character seems limited and lifeless. Pseudo-Dionysius is a help here also. He searches all of Scripture for the many names for God and expands what later came to be a somewhat limited conversation. Two of his favorite names for God are light and beauty. Because he is talking about divine simplicity, the light and beauty of God are the goodness of God, which is also the wisdom of God, for the traits are like facets of a diamond. "Light comes from the Good, light is an image of this archetypal Good. . . . It gives light to everything capable of receiving it; it creates them, keeps them alive, preserves and perfects them. Everything looks to it for measure, eternity, number, order. It is the power that embraces the universe. It is the Cause of the universe and its end."[15]

Beauty also names God:

> In itself and by itself it is the uniquely and the eternally beautiful. It is the superabundant source in itself of the beauty of every beautiful thing. In that simple but transcendent nature of all beautiful things, beauty and the beautiful uniquely preexisted in terms of their source. From this beauty comes the existence of everything, each being exhibiting in its own way of beauty. For beauty is the cause of harmony, of sympathy, of community. Beauty unites all things and is the source of all things. It is the great creating cause which bestirs the world and holds all things in existence by the longing inside them to have beauty.[16]

In sum, Pseudo-Dionysius finds divine simplicity not only dynamic but also multivalent and therefore spiritually seductive, if I may be permitted an unusual turn of phrase.

If God's character is presented as dynamic, multivalent, and teeming with life as discerned through creation, it is more difficult to perceive it as remote and lifeless. God's character was certainly not lifeless for Dionysius or for any other Christian Platonist, for that matter. They all believed that we can and do participate in God's character and benefit from it through revelation, not speculation. One reason the divine simplicity was appealing is that although they appreciated the dynamism of God, they also longed for relief from personal struggle and sought rest in God's stability; rest was not alienating but appealing, as I think it might be to postmoderns struggling to recover from the fragmentation of the self and the loss of moral stability. Another reason the divine simplicity was appealing is that they did not radically disjoin us humans from God—the instances of God's character convey Godness itself, with its multivalence, to us.

Conclusion

The concern raised here is that the new trinitarian orthodoxy, in its desire to extirpate residual Greek elements from Christian doctrine, may deprive us of the ability to be transformed by the goodness, wisdom, and beauty of God. Defining God by the economy alone nails our salvation to specific events or acts whereas our God-given ability to grow beyond sinfulness demands that we become wiser, more beautiful, and more righteous than heretofore through the process of knowing and loving God, which itself transforms the sin-sick soul. The preceding discussion is offered to remind radical trinitarians of the soteriological value of the divine perfections, which pertain to us and give us hope for our future.

9

Deep Wisdom

CORNELIUS PLANTINGA JR.

[Jesus] looked up to heaven and said: "Father, the hour has come; glorify your Son so that your Son may glorify you." (John 17:1)

The glory that you have given me I have given them, so that they may be one, as we are one. (John 17:22)

Brothers and sisters in Jesus Christ: Viktor Klemperer was professor of literature at the University of Dresden in the years that led into World War II, and he had the job he wanted. All his life he had loved to read and write, and all his life he had dreamed of writing a definitive account of eighteenth-century French literature. If he succeeded, he would be eminent throughout academe and thus could hold his head up in the faculty lounge. At learned conferences he could autograph his book, and he could do it graciously and illegibly. He would be a master in his field! Anybody who wanted to talk about eighteenth-century French literature would have to talk about Viktor Klemperer. How satisfying all this would be for him!

But then the Nazis came to power and started removing one part of Klemperer's life after another. They took away his telephone and then his car. They canceled some of his courses at the university, and then they canceled all of them. The Nazis removed his typewriter and then took away his house and gave it to a local grocer. The grocer was actually opposed to Hitler, but he was still pleased to have Klemperer's house. The Nazis moved Klemperer into a so-called Jews' House, which was normally the last stop on the way to the camps, and they also killed Klemperer's cat because they did not allow Jews to own pets.

As the Nazis robbed him, Klemperer wrote it all down in his diary. He wrote about his deprivations and the indignities that came with them. He described tyranny and what it did to people—how it made some of them largehearted and compassionate, and how it made others tight and self-protective. In 1941, after a terrifying run-in with the police, Klemperer opened his diary and wrote these words: "I want to bear witness, precise witness, until the very end." He knew that in his confinement he could not write a big history of Nazi cruelty. But he could tell his diary about the ordinary ways the Nazis stripped people of their dignity, right down to the last rag of it.

Viktor Klemperer had hoped to write the world's best account of eighteenth-century French literature. But the Nazis took his life away. Except that, at the end of the day, they didn't. They couldn't. The reason is that Viktor Klemperer's diaries survived and are now celebrated all over the world. One day my friend Eleonore Stump pointed all this out to me. Klemperer had thought that his glory would be a book about French literature, but the Lord meant his glory to be his daily diary. Viktor Klemperer could not stop the Nazis from robbing him, but there was one thing he could do. He could "bear witness, precise witness," and he could "bear it to the end." He was a martyr for the truth, and he never knew that *this* would be his glory. He was like Moses coming down the mountain from God with his face shining, but without *knowing* that his face was shining.

How hard it is to see real glory. How hard to see real glory when we think glory is all about making a splash. We miss the real thing because we borrow our standards from people who have mixed glory up with publicity—people like pro athletes and entertainers, hard-charging winners in politics and business, occupants of named chairs in departments of literature. Some folks think there is glory in being lethal, or sexist, or profane.

James Alison wrote a book about this. In ordinary life, glory is reputation. It is reputation built on competition and publicity and peer review by people just as screwed up as we are.

So once more the Bible must be our teacher because it finds glory somewhere else and usually in places where we are not looking for it. You thought you would go for some lunch, as Barbara Brown Taylor writes: you are out to lunch, and all of a sudden God "smacks you upside the head with glory."[1] God's glory has nothing to do with competition or publicity. It has to do with something else.

In John 2 Jesus goes to a wedding, and his mother reports a wine shortage, so Jesus goes to work. He makes some wine. In fact, he makes a lot of wine, plenty of wine, maybe 150 gallons or so (must have been a large wedding). When it comes to making wine, Jesus has an advantage over other vintners because he is the one through whom everything was made in the beginning. Jesus knows his business, and so he makes very good wine, special reserve wine that bursts with fruit and makes everybody's heart glad indeed. The Gospel says it is a sign of his glory (v. 11). We want to know what this mysterious glory is, and why we should see it in winemaking.

The Fourth Gospel finds glory in places where we are not looking. In John 12 death is in the air. The Son of Man will die and fall into the earth in an event so devastating that it will seem to turn creation back into chaos, but Jesus says that this is the hour in which the Son of Man will be *glorified* (v. 23). We grope for his meaning. The men and women who loved Jesus would see him die on a torture instrument that the Romans had adapted to terrorize their enemies. They would see the Romans take his life, and before that they would see the Romans take his dignity in a public spectacle meant to intimidate anybody with an eye to see or an ear to hear or a heart to tremble at state-sponsored terrorism and the awful suffering it brings. The Romans jammed their crosses into the earth like scarecrows, and every damned one of them proclaimed to the world, "Caesar is Lord, and don't you ever forget it."

"The hour has come for the Son of Man to be *glorified*," says Jesus. How can this be? Being glorified on a cross? Is that like being enthroned on an electric chair? Is it like being honored by a firing squad?

Glory in the cross of Jesus Christ sounds almost grotesque. After all, as Jürgen Moltmann once wrote, Jesus was crucified "not between two candles on an altar, but between two thieves in the place of the skull."[2] Jesus, the friend of sinners, was crucified between his kind of people in a godforsaken place where all the lights go out from noon to three. And yet the Gospel wants us to find glory in this disaster, and we want to know what this mysterious glory is, and why we should see it in Jesus's terrible suffering.

I say the Gospel finds glory in places where we are not looking for it. Glory in the wine of Jesus and in the blood of Jesus, and one more glory. The Gospel tells us that the same Jesus who knew he was going to die, the same Jesus whose soul was storming and heaving, this deeply troubled man, once did something his disciples talked about for years. John 13 tells us that one night when Jesus's hour had come, he took off his robe, tied a towel around himself, poured water into a basin, and bent over the feet of his disciples. Jesus did for them what they would never have dreamed of doing for each other, and he apparently did it for Judas too. He also handed Judas bread—*feeding* the traitor, feeding the traitor with *bread*, which has always been the signal of God's enthusiasm for a human life. According to the Gospel, when Judas took these gifts from Jesus and walked out into the darkness with them, Jesus said, "Now the Son of Man has been glorified, and *God* has been glorified in him" (13:31). Once more we want to know what this mysterious glory is all about, and why we should find it in the washing and the feeding.

Glory is everywhere in the Gospel, and it has nothing to do with competition or making a splash. The glory is in wine and blood. It is in bread and bathwater. It is where we are not looking, but it is certainly where Jesus is, and God is also mixed up in the glory because the Son just does what his Father does. He just says what his Father says. The Son is his Father all over again.

By the way, as if this isn't glory and mystery enough, there is also a third party in the picture, the *paraklētos*, the Advocate, actually the second Advocate, who fills in when Jesus goes away. Chapters 14–16 tell us about the second Advocate, who stays with the disciples to remind them of Jesus, to glorify Jesus, to bear witness to the truth about Jesus. The Spirit of Truth bears witness, precise witness, and bears it to the end.

If even this is not mystery and glory enough, sisters and brothers, think with me now about what our Lord says in chapter 17. Which of us has enough depth or wisdom to hold this magisterial prayer? Who has even the right tone to voice it? Who has mind or heart enough for it? I know I don't.

But I do know this. All the glory we have been wondering about—the glory in wine and blood and water and bread—all the glory that shines out in the neighborhood of Jesus and God and the Holy Spirit—this mysterious glory also shines out from the prayer, and from Jesus who offers it. Maybe for the few minutes left to us; maybe if we behold his glory, the glory of the one and only from the Father; maybe then our own faces will start to shine a little, and we can go home like Moses coming down the mountain.

In John 17 Jesus's hour has come. He's only one chapter from the place where Judas and the soldiers will meet him with their torches and weapons, and what does Jesus do? He prays for his disciples. He thinks of *them* and prays for *them*. He thinks even of the next generation of disciples who will be gathered through evangelism, and he prays for them too. "Protect them," he prays. "Holy Father, protect them. Sanctify them. Unite them. Fill them with joy. Let me be in them, and you in me, and they in us. Let your love, which has been my own life's blood from before the foundation of the world—let your love be in them and I in them, and in all the generations who will believe the gospel."

The Gospel says that after Jesus speaks these words, he goes out to the garden to meet Judas and the soldiers and to drink the cup the Father has given him.

Holy Father, protect them. Unite them. Love them. Fill them with joy. The prayer is thrilling in its courage and beauty—thrilling, hair-raising, overwhelming in its courage and beauty. Jesus pours himself out for his disciples while his own life hangs by a thread, and in this, sisters and brothers, in this we behold his glory, glory as of the one and only from the Father, full of grace and truth. Here is the *plērōma* of grace, the fullness of grace, grace upon grace, always out to bless, always out to adorn, to unite, to cause others to flourish, always thinking of others, doing whatever it takes, paying whatever it costs, the Son of God going flat out in grace and truth so that others may live and do so abundantly.

Where did Jesus get all this? He received some of it from his mother, we claim, the fierce and blessed Virgin Mary. Jesus was his mother's Son. He received some of it from the Holy Spirit, who conceived him and descended upon him and remained with him. And certainly, from all eternity Jesus Christ, the Son of God, the Word of God, the light of God—from all eternity Jesus Christ received his glorious self-giving habits from being in the bosom of his Father, who is the overflowing fountain of divinity, the One whose greatness consists so much in his goodness.

So Jesus just does what he sees his Father doing. Jesus makes lots of wine at Cana because he comes from a winemaking family. Every fall God turns water into wine in France and Chile and the Napa Valley. Gregory the Great said that at Cana Jesus just did a small, speeded-up version of what God does all the time in the great vineyards of the world. Jesus makes wine for people because they're at a wedding, and he wants them to flourish there. He wants to make their joy full.

Glory in the wine of Jesus, and glory in the washbasin of Jesus. Hasn't God always humbled himself to serve us, even when our sin has led us into terrible trouble? "Have mercy on me, O God, according to your steadfast love; according to your abundant mercy blot out my transgressions. Wash me thoroughly from my iniquity, and cleanse me from my sin" (Ps. 51:1–2). Jesus on his knees before his disciples is just doing what he sees his Father doing, and of course the Gospel finds glory here because it is so much like God to clean people up and cause them to flourish.

And bread for a traitor? Doesn't God do this all the time—sending rain on the fields of the just and the unjust so that their crops will grow and they will grow too as they feed on God's gifts? Jesus hands Judas a piece of bread because he just does what he sees his Father doing, and the Gospel finds glory here because it is so much like God to feed enemies and cause them to flourish even while you oppose their evil.

I say the Gospel finds glory where we are not looking, in the wine, and the water, and the bread, and even in the blood of Jesus our Savior. How grotesque it seems to us that the Gospel should find glory in Jesus's crucifixion. He is lifted up on a cross, almost as if it is the first five feet of his ascension into heaven. But the glory is in it, because God's love is all over it. "God so loved the world that he gave his one and only Son" (John 3:16

NIV). I hope we hear the passion in these words. People think that love means the willingness to share feelings. Love is exercising the option to communicate. But love like this won't take anybody to a cross.

To go to a cross for somebody, your love would have to be fierce. To go to a cross you would have to be terrifying in the strength of your passion for sinners. "God so loved the world that he sent his only Son"—that's not just a Bible verse. That's a cry from the depths. That's almost a battle cry.

In the mystery of the cross, the humiliating death of Jesus Christ was actually a triumph of self-giving love, "the atoning sacrifice for . . . the sins of the whole world" (1 John 2:2). That is why it brings glory to God. The point is that God's splendor becomes clearer whenever God or the Son of God powerfully spends himself in order to cause others to flourish. Here is the glory. Here is the power and the glory.

From all eternity inside God, inside the mystery of God, inside God the Holy Trinity—the Father and the Son and the Holy Spirit make room for each other, envelop each other, call attention to each other, glorify one another. It is the ceaseless exchange of vitality, the endless expense of spirit upon spirit in eternal triplicate life. The only competition in glory of this kind is to outdo one another in love.

For us, brothers and sisters, this is deep wisdom: we find our flourishing only in causing others to flourish. This is eternal life: to receive this wisdom from God and from Jesus, whom God has sent. How astonishing it is to know that when we help others to thrive, when we encourage them, strengthen them, liberate them, keep our promises to them—how astonishing it is to know that when we do these things, we are like God!

We thought we would gain glory by writing a terrific book or receiving a strong peer review from people just as foolish as we are. But the Spirit of truth tells us the real glory is in the wine and the blood and the water and the bread, and maybe that's a truth about God the Holy Trinity that we can take down the mountain with us today, our faces shining from God's love.

In the name of the Father and of the Son and of the Holy Spirit. Amen.

Notes

Introduction

1. Ralph Del Colle, "The Triune God," in *Cambridge Companion to Christian Doctrine*, ed. Colin E. Gunton (Cambridge: Cambridge University Press, 1997), 134.

2. Jaroslav Pelikan, *Historical Theology: Continuity and Change in Christian Doctrine* (Philadelphia: Westminster, 1971), 160.

3. Karl Barth, *Church Dogmatics*, 14 vols. in 5 (Edinburgh: T&T Clark, 1936–77).

4. See Karl Rahner, *Theological Investigations*, 23 vols. (Baltimore: Helicon, et al., 1961–92), 1:79–148, 319–46; 4:105–20.

5. Alister E. McGrath, *Christian Theology* (Oxford: Blackwell, 2001), 337.

Chapter 1: The Doctrine of the Trinity

1. Lewis Carroll, *Through the Looking Glass* (London: Macmillan, 1871), chap. 5.

2. Alasdair MacIntyre, *Three Rival Versions of Moral Enquiry: Encyclopaedia, Genealogy, and Tradition*, Gifford Lectures 1987–88 (Notre Dame, IN: University of Notre Dame Press, 1990).

3. Augustine, *Serm.* 117: "If you understand him, he is not God."

4. Bruno Latour, *We Have Never Been Modern* (Cambridge, MA: Harvard University Press, 1993), 10.

5. Leonardo Boff, *Trinity and Society* (London: Burns & Oates, 1988), 159.

6. Enrico De Negri, *Offenbarung und Dialektik: Luthers Realtheologie* (Darmstadt: Wissenschaftliche Buchgesellschaft, 1973); Alister E. McGrath, *Luther's Theology of the Cross: Martin Luther's Theological Breakthrough* (Oxford: Blackwell, 1985), 148–75.

7. There is a huge amount of literature on Gestalt theory, ably summarized in Barry Smith, *Austrian Philosophy: The Legacy of Franz Brentano* (Chicago: Open Court, 1994), 255–311.

8. Hans Urs von Balthasar, *Herrlichkeit: Eine theologische Ästhetik*, vol. 1, *Schau der Gestalt* (Einsiedeln: Johannes Verlag, 1961), 290. Von Balthasar often uses the term *Ganzheit* as a synonym for *Gestalt*, bringing out this aspect of "an irreducible totality"; see Mantred Lochbrunner, *Analogia caritatis: Darstellung und Deutung der Theologie Hans Urs von Balthasars* (Freiburg: Herder, 1981), 173. Concerning von Balthasar on the related issue of "singularity," see Jörg Peter Disse, *Metaphysik der Singularität: Eine Hinführung am Leitfaden der Philosophie Hans Urs von Balthasars* (Vienna: Passagen-Verlag, 1996).

9. Von Balthasar, *Herrlichkeit*, 144–45.

10. For what follows, see especially the 1949–50 Gifford Lectures: Gabriel Marcel, *The Mystery of Being* (London: Harvill, 1950). He also develops the distinction in his earlier work: idem, *Être et avoir* (Paris: Aubier/Montaigne, 1935). For studies of Marcel's approach, see Roger Troisfontaines, *De l'existence à l'être: La philosophie de Gabriel Marcel*, 2 vols. (Louvain: Nauwelaerts, 1953); Giuseppe Russo, *Gabriel Marcel: esistenza e partecipazione* (Battipaglia: Il Fedone, 1993).

11. Austin Farrer, *The Glass of Vision* (London: Dacre, 1948), 64–78. Farrer explicitly acknowledges his debt to Marcel at this point: *The Glass of Vision*, x–xi.

12. Ibid., 65–66.

13. Ibid., 67.

14. Ibid., 72.

15. Charles Gore, *The Incarnation of the Son of God* (London: John Murray, 1922), 105–6.

16. E.g., see John R. W. Stott, *The Bible: Book for Today* (Leicester: Inter-Varsity, 1982), 36.

17. E.g., see John R. W. Stott, *The Lausanne Covenant: An Exposition and Commentary* (Minneapolis: World Wide Publications, 1975), 5.

18. E.g., see John R. W. Stott, *The Authentic Jesus* (Downers Grove, IL: InterVarsity, 1985), 9.

19. For some reflections, see Alister E. McGrath, *Evangelicalism and the Future of Christianity* (Downers Grove, IL: InterVarsity, 1995); John R. W. Stott, *Evangelical Truth* (Leicester: Inter-Varsity, 1999); K. S. Kantzer and C. F. H. Henry, *Evangelical Affirmations* (Grand Rapids: Zondervan, 1990); George M. Marsden, *Reforming Fundamentalism: Fuller Seminary and the New Evangelicalism* (Grand Rapids: Eerdmans, 1987). In the Canadian context, see especially John G. Stackhouse, *Canadian Evangelicalism in the Twentieth Century: An Introduction to Its Character* (Toronto: University of Toronto Press, 1993).

20. For a useful study of the issues, see Arthur William Wainwright, *The Trinity in the New Testament* (London: SPCK, 1962). For an older but still useful study, see Jules Lebreton, *The Living God: The Revelation of the Holy Trinity in the New Testament* (London: Faith, 1923). More generally, see Thomas G. Weinandy, *The Father's Spirit of Sonship: Reconceiving the Trinity* (Edinburgh: T&T Clark, 1995).

21. I explore this in *A Passion for Truth: The Intellectual Coherence of Evangelicalism* (Downers Grove, IL: InterVarsity, 1996), 10–20. The best discussion

of this aspect of evangelicalism known to me is Richard J. Mouw, *Consulting the Faithful: What Christian Intellectuals Can Learn from Popular Religion* (Grand Rapids: Eerdmans, 1994).

22. See Brian Leftow, "Anti Social Trinitarianism," in Stephen T. Davis, Daniel Kendall, and Gerald O'Collins, eds., *The Trinity: An Interdisciplinary Symposium on the Doctrine of the Trinity* (Oxford: Oxford University Press, 1999), 203–49.

23. Leonardo Boff, *Trinity and Society* (London: Burns & Oates, 1988). For further exploration, see Thomas D. Parker, "The Political Meaning of the Doctrine of the Trinity: Some Theses," *Journal of Religion* 60 (1980): 165–84.

24. Parker, "Political Meaning," 182.

25. Jürgen Moltmann, *The Trinity and the Kingdom of God: The Doctrine of God* (London: SCM, 1981).

26. Ibid., 215.

27. For more detailed discussion, see Sarah Coakley, "'Persons' in the 'Social' Doctrine of the Trinity," in Davis et al., *The Trinity*, 123–44.

28. For what follows, see Robert W. Jenson, *The Triune Identity: God according to the Gospel* (Philadelphia: Fortress, 1982). On this important work, see further Colin E. Gunton, *Trinity, Time, and Church: A Response to the Theology of Robert W. Jenson* (Grand Rapids: Eerdmans, 2000).

29. Thomas à Kempis, *De imitatione Christi* 1.1–2; in *De imitatione Christi libri quatuor*, ed. T. Lupo (Vatican City: Libreria Editrice Vaticana, 1982), 4–8.

Chapter 3: Faith and Christian Life in the African-American Spirituals

1. See Jon Michael Spencer, *Black Hymnody: A Hymnological History of the African American Church* (Knoxville: University of Tennessee Press, 1992). John Lovell Jr., writing on the contemporary use of the gospel music genre in the Black church, has explained: "What is called gospel music is hardly anything more than an effort to give the spiritual a modernity in form, content, and beat." See his *Black Song: The Forge and the Flame* (New York: Paragon House, 1972), 467.

2. See Howard Thurman, *With Head and Heart: The Autobiography of Howard Thurman* (New York: Harcourt Brace Jovanovitch, 1979), 216; idem, *The Negro Spiritual Speaks of Life and Death: Being the Ingersoll Lecture on the Immortality of Man, 1947* (New York: Harper & Brothers, 1947), 12.

3. See Alain Locke, "The Negro Spirituals," in *The New Negro: An Interpretation* (New York: Borsi, 1925), 199–210; idem, repr. in *Freedom on My Mind: The Columbia Documentary History of the African American Experience*, ed. Manning Marable (New York: Columbia University Press, 2003), esp. 587.

4. W. E. B. DuBois, *The Souls of Black Folk*, ed. Henry Louis Gates and Terri Hume Oliver, Norton Critical Edition (New York: Norton, 1999), esp. 154–64.

5. Booker T. Washington, "Preface" to *Twenty-Four Negro Melodies: Transcribed for the Piano by Samuel Coleridge-Taylor* (Bryn Mawr, PA: Oliver Ditson, 1905), viii.

6. Miles Mark Fisher, *Negro Slave Songs in the United States* (New York: Citadel, 1953).

7. Lovell, *Black Song*.

8. See Thomas Carlyle's essay on "The Hero as a Poet," in *Heroes, Hero-Worship, and the Heroic in History*, ed. Archibald MacMechan (Boston: Ginn, 1901), 95.

9. Thurman, *Negro Spiritual Speaks of Life and Death*, 12.

10. Cited from the preface, Benjamin E. Mays, *The Negro's God: As Reflected in His Literature* (1938; repr., New York: Atheneum, 1969), with a new preface by Vincent Harding.

11. Ibid., 21.

12. "Go Down, Moses," in *The Books of American Negro Spirituals*, compiled by James Weldon Johnson and J. Rosamond Johnson (New York: Viking, 1969), 1:51–53.

13. "Joshua Fit de Battle ob Jericho," in Johnson, *Books of American Negro Spirituals*, 1:56–58.

14. Lovell, *Black Song*, 229.

15. "Didn't My Lord Deliver Daniel?" in Johnson, *Books of American Negro Spirituals*, 1:148–51.

16. "God Is a God! God Don't Never Change," in Lovell, *Black Song*, 238.

17. "He Never Said a Mumbalin' Word," in ibid., 261.

18. Johnson, *Books of American Negro Spirituals*, 2:136–37.

19. Thurman, *With Head and Heart*, 134.

20. "But He Ain't Comin' Here t' Die No Mo'," in *Religious Folk-Songs of the Negro: As Sung at Hampton*, ed. R. Nathaniel Dett (Hampton, VA: Hampton Institute Press, 1927), 103.

21. "Dust an' Ashes," in ibid., 213–18.

22. "'Tis Me," in ibid., 183.

23. "Lord, I Want to Be a Christian," in ibid., 50–51.

24. "I'm Troubled in Mind," in ibid., 236.

25. "Jesus Goin' to Make Up My Dying Bed," in Lovell, *Black Song*, 319.

26. Henry H. Mitchell, *Black Belief: Folk Beliefs of Blacks in America and West Africa* (New York: Harper & Row, 1975), 130.

27. "Dere's a Little Wheel a-Turnin' in My Heart," in Dett, *Religious Folk-Songs*, 168.

28. "I Know the Lord's Laid His Hands on Me," in ibid., 207.

29. "Ev'ry Time I Feel the Spirit," in ibid., 169.

30. "There Is a Balm in Gilead," in ibid., 88.

31. "Done Made My Vow to the Lord," in Lovell, *Black Song*, 323.

Chapter 4: The Trinity and Christian Unity

1. Augustine, *Ennarr Ps.* 32 [33], in sermon 2, sec. 29; in CCSL 38:272–73. I have followed the translation in the *Liturgy of the Hours* for Tuesday of the 14th Week of the Year. In referring to the "prophet," Augustine is alluding to Isa. 66:5 LXX.

2. Augustine, *Serm.* 71:33; PL 38:463–64. Here I have adapted the English translation in *The Works of St. Augustine: A Translation for the 21st Century*, trans. Edmund Hill, O.P., vol. 3, *Sermons on the New Testament*, nos. 51–94 (Brooklyn, NY: New City Press, 1991), 266–67.

3. Tertullian, *Bapt.* 6; ANF 3:672, translation modified.

4. Cyprian, *De or.* 23; CSEL IIIA, p. 285; ANF 5:454.

5. Thomas Aquinas, *Summa theologiae* III, qu. 48, art. 2, ad 1, and elsewhere. See Heribert Mühlen, *Una mystica persona* (Munich: Schöningh, 1968), 40–44.

6. Bruno Forte, *The Church: Icon of the Trinity* (Boston: St. Paul Books & Media, 1991). We may regard this little book as a sketch of his later work, *La chiesa della Trinità* (Milan: San Paolo, 1995).

7. This is the famous thesis proposed by Erik Peterson in 1935 and still upheld, I believe, as substantially accurate, though some historical problems must be raised.

8. Cardinal Joseph Ratzinger, *Church, Ecumenism, and Politics* (New York: Crossroad, 1988), 31–32. The views of Soloviev are helpfully summarized in Egbert Munzer, *Solovyev: Prophet of Russian-Western Unity* (London: Hollis & Carter, 1956).

9. Miroslav Volf, *After Our Likeness: The Church as the Image of the Trinity* (Grand Rapids: Eerdmans, 1998), 217, citing Jürgen Moltmann, *Geist des Lebens: Ganzheitliche Pneumatologie* (Munich: Kaiser, 1991), 323.

10. Jürgen Moltmann, *The Trinity and the Kingdom* (San Francisco: Harper & Row, 1981), 176.

11. Miroslav Volf, "Trinity, Unity, Primacy: On the Trinitarian Nature of Unity and Its Implications for the Question of Primacy," in *Petrine Ministry and the Unity of the Church*, ed. James F. Puglisi (Collegeville, MN: Liturgical Press, 1999), 171–84, esp. 179.

12. Ibid., 178.

13. Ratzinger, *Church, Ecumenism, and Politics*, 34, 36.

14. Ignatius of Antioch, *Magn.* 6.1; ANF 1:61.

15. Ignatius of Antioch, *Smyrn.* 8.1; ANF 1:89.

16. Ignatius of Antioch, *Rom.*, inscr.; ANF 1:73.

17. Irenaeus, *Haer.* 3.3.2; ANF 1:415.

18. Thomas Aquinas, *Contra errores graecorum*, chap. 32.

19. Yves Congar, *Ministères et communion ecclésiale* (Paris: Cerf, 1971), 101–2.

20. Forte, *La chiesa della Trinità*, 265–66.

21. Louis Bouyer, *The Church of God* (Chicago: Franciscan Herald Press, 1982), 278–79.

22. On this subject see especially J.-M. R. Tillard, *Église d'églises* (Paris: Cerf, 1987); and idem, *L'église locale: Ecclésiologie de communion et de catholicité* (Paris: Cerf, 1995). Using *koinōnia* as his key concept, Tillard thinks of each particular church as a "communion" and of the universal church as a "communion of communions." See his *Églises d'églises*, 101; ET, *Church of Churches: The Ecclesiology of Communion* (Collegeville, MN: Liturgical Press, 1992), 74.

23. Vatican II, Lumen gentium 26; idem, Sacrosanctum Concilium 41; idem, Christus Dominus 11.

24. On the nature of ecclesial *typoi*, see Jan Cardinal Willebrands, Address at Great St. Mary's Church, Cambridge, England, January 18, 1970, in *Documents on Anglican/Roman Catholic Relations* (Washington, DC: United States Catholic Conference, 1972), 32–41.

25. The Nairobi Report of the World Council of Churches states: "It is because the unity of the Church is grounded in the divine triunity that we can speak of

diversity in the Church as something to be not only admitted but actively desired." See "Report of Section II: What Unity Requires," §7, in *Breaking Barriers: Nairobi 1975*, ed. David M. Paton (Grand Rapids: Eerdmans, 1976), 61.

26. Ibid., §§2–6, pp. 60–61.

27. Ibid., §4.

Chapter 6: A Puritan Perspective

1. See works on the life of Owen. The best are by Andrew Thomson, *Works of John Owen*, ed. William H. Goold (Edinburgh: Johnstone & Hunter, 1850–53), 1:xxi–cxii (repr., London: Banner of Truth, 1965–68); and Peter Toon, *God's Statesman* (Exeter: Paternoster, 1971).

2. See John Owen, *The Reason of Faith* (1677); and idem, *The Causes, Ways and Means of Understanding the Mind of God as Revealed in His Word* (1678); both in *Works*, vol. 4. Also see idem, *Of the Divine Original, Authority, Self-Evidencing Light, and Power of the Scriptures* (1659); and idem, *Of the Integrity and Purity of the Hebrew and Greek Text of the Scriptures* (1659); both in *Works*, vol. 16.

3. See Owen, *Theologoumena pantodapa*, in Latin (1661), in *Works*, vol. 17; ET, *Biblical Theology*, trans. Stephen P. Westcott (Pittsburgh: Soli Deo Gloria, 1994).

4. See Owen, *Christologia* (1679); and idem, *Meditations and Discourses on the Glory of Christ* (1684/1691); both in *Works*, vol. 1.

5. See Owen, *Pneumatologia* (1674), in *Works*, vol. 3; and idem, the smaller treatises in *Works*, vol. 4: *The Reason of Faith*; *Causes, Ways and Means* (see note 2 above); *Of the Work of the Holy Spirit in Prayer* (1682); and *Two Discourses concerning the Holy Spirit and His Work: The One, Of The Spirit as a Comforter; the Other, As He Is the Author of Spiritual Gifts* (1693).

6. Owen, *Works*, vol. 5.

7. See the many compositions contained in Owen, *Works*, vols. 13–16. Idem, *The True Nature of a Gospel Church* (1689), in *Works*, vol. 16, is a classic statement of Congregational polity.

8. See Owen, *Of Communion with God the Father, Son, and Holy Ghost* (1657), in *Works*, vol. 2; and idem, *The Grace and Duty of Being Spiritually Minded* (1681), in *Works*, vol. 7.

9. See Owen, *Of the Mortification of Sin in Believers* (1656); and idem, *The Nature, Power, Deceit, and Prevalency of the Remainders of Indwelling Sin in Believers* (1668); both in *Works*, vol. 6.

10. See Owen, *The Doctrine of the Saints' Perseverance* (1654), in *Works*, vol. 11; idem, *A Practical Exposition upon Psalm 130* (1668), in *Works*, vol. 6; idem, *Evidences of the Faith of God's Elect* (1695), in *Works*, vol. 5; idem, *The Nature of Apostasy* (1676), in *Works*, vol. 7.

11. Owen, *Works*, vols. 18–24.

12. Sinclair B. Ferguson, *John Owen on the Christian Life* (Edinburgh: Banner of Truth, 1987), 18.

13. The heavy, roundabout style is the same in Owen's letters: see his *Works*, 1:ci–ciii, cxiv–cxxi; Peter Toon, *Correspondence of John Owen* (Cambridge: James Clarke, 1970).

14. Owen, *Works*, 12:52.

15. Ibid., 6:4.

16. On Ramism and its influence, see Perry Miller, *The New England Mind: The Seventeenth Century* (Cambridge, MA: Harvard University Press, 1939), 11–53; W. J. Ong, *Ramus, Method, and the Decay of Dialogue* (Cambridge, MA: Harvard University Press, 1958); K. L. Sprunger, "Ames, Ramus, and the Method of Puritan Theology," *Harvard Theological Review* 59 (1966): 133–51; W. M. Kneale and J. Kneale, *The Development of Logic* (Oxford: Clarendon, 1962), 301ff.

17. On this see Edward Farley, *Theologia* (Philadelphia: Fortress, 1983); Ellen T. Charry, *By the Renewing of Your Minds: The Pastoral Function of Christian Theology* (New York: Oxford University Press, 1997); J. I. Packer, "Theology and Wisdom," in *The Way of Wisdom*, ed. J. I. Packer and Sven K. Soderlund (Grand Rapids: Zondervan, 2001); John Owen, *Biblical Theology*, 6:9, 685–703.

18. In Owen, *Works*, 10:1ff., 139ff. The full title of the latter is worth noting: *Salus Electorum, Sanguis Jesu; or, The Death of Death in the Death of Christ: A Treatise of the Redemption and Reconciliation that is in the Blood of Christ; with the Merit thereof, and the Satisfaction wrought thereby: Wherein the Proper End of the Death of Christ is Asserted; the Immediate Effects and Fruits thereof Assigned, with their Extent in respect of its Object; and the Whole Controversy about Universal Redemption Fully Discussed.* Owen liked to give his major works Latin or Greek main titles, presumably to lay claim to full academic quality.

19. A flow of distinguished books and articles by Richard A. Muller effectively challenges this fancy: see especially his *Post-Reformation Reformed Dogmatics*, 2 vols. (Grand Rapids: Baker, 1987–93).

20. Carl R. Trueman, *The Claims of Truth: John Owen's Trinitarian Theology* (Carlisle: Paternoster, 1998).

21. Ibid., 12.

22. Ibid., 18.

23. These words appear unchanged in the Savoy Declaration of 1658, the consensus statement of England's Congregational Independents. Owen was a major drafter of the Savoy Declaration, which is modeled on the Westminster Confession.

24. Owen, *Works*, 2:2–274.

25. Ibid., 2:3.

26. From Owen, *A Brief Declaration and Vindication of the Doctrine of the Trinity* (1669), in *Works*, 2:377.

27. Owen, *Vindiciae evangelicae*, in *Works*, vol. 12. The work by John Biddle was *A Twofold Catechism* (London: J. Cottrel for R. Moone, 1654).

28. See John 3:16–17; 6:35–46; 10:1–18; chap. 17 passim.

29. Owen, *Works*, 2:8–9.

30. Ibid., 2:16.

31. Trueman, *Claims of Truth*, 83.

32. Owen, *Works*, 2:44.

33. Ibid., 2:77–78.

34. Ibid., 2:31. "Alters he not his love towards them? Not the *purpose* of this will, but the *dispensations* of his grace. He *rebukes* them, he *chastens* them, he *hides* his face from them, he *smites* them, he fills them with a sense of his *indignation*; but woe, woe would it be to us, should he change in his love, or take

away his kindness from us!" Owen cites Ps. 39:11; Heb. 12:7–8; Rev. 3:19; Isa. 8:17; 57:17; Job 6:4; Pss. 6:6; 38:3–5.

35. Ibid., 2:34.

36. Ibid., 2:36.

37. Ibid., 2:243: "The Holy Ghost communicates unto us his own likeness; which is also the image of the Father and the Son."

38. Ibid., 2:242.

39. Ibid., 2:244, 246.

40. Ibid., 2:270–72.

41. Amy Plantinga Pauw, *The Supreme Harmony of All: The Trinitarian Theology of Jonathan Edwards* (Grand Rapids: Eerdmans, 2002), 5–7; Janice Knight, *Orthodoxies in Massachusetts: Rereading American Puritanism* (Cambridge, MA: Harvard University Press, 1994).

42. Pauw, *Supreme Harmony of All*, 5.

43. American Puritanism was English Puritanism exported, mutated structurally in the new colonial situation, but theologically and pastorally unchanged.

44. See Owen, *Of the Work of the Holy Spirit as a Comforter*, a posthumous publication in *Works*, vol. 4; it is simply a restatement of key thoughts from the treatise *Of Communion* (1657).

45. Owen, *Works*, 2:2.

Chapter 7: The Trinity and the Challenge of Islam

1. *The Koran*, trans. N. J. Dawood (London: Penguin, 1999), 372.

2. Kenneth Cragg, *The Call of the Minaret* (New York: Oxford University Press, 1956), 31, 35–41.

3. Philipp Melanchthon, in the introduction to the first edition of his *Loci communes* (1521; 2nd ed. of repr. in Latin and German, Gütersloh: G. Mohn, 1997).

4. George Eliot, *Silas Marner* (New York: Harper & Brothers, 1861).

5. Cragg, *Call of the Minaret*, 288.

6. Thomas Hardy, *The Dynasts*, part 3, in *Verse*, vol. 2, in *The Works of Thomas Hardy in Prose and Verse* (London: Macmillan, 1913), 254.

7. Arthur Chute McGill, *Suffering: A Test of Theological Method* (Philadelphia: Westminster, 1982).

Chapter 8: The Soteriological Importance of the Divine Perfections

1. Suggestions for a new ontology have come from Robert W. Jenson, *The Triune Identity: God according to the Gospel* (Philadelphia: Fortress, 1982); Jürgen Moltmann, *The Trinity and the Kingdom of God: The Doctrine of God* (London: SCM, 1981); Catherine M. LaCugna, *God for Us: The Trinity and Christian Life* (San Francisco: Harper, 1991); and John D. Zizioulas, *Being as Communion: Studies in Personhood and the Church* (Crestwood, NY: St. Vladimir's Seminary Press, 1985).

2. Karen Kilby, "Perichoresis and Projection: Problems with Social Doctrines of the Trinity," *New Blackfriars* 81 (2000): 432–45, citation at 433.

3. Adolf von Harnack, *History of Dogma* (New York: Dover, 1961), 129–30.

4. See Karl Barth, *Church Dogmatics*, 14 vols. in 5 (Edinburgh: T&T Clark, 1936–77), II/1:323–677.

5. Phillip Cary, *Augustine's Invention of the Inner Self: The Legacy of a Christian Platonist* (New York: Oxford University Press, 2000).

6. Augustine, *The Trinity*, trans. Edmund Hill (Brooklyn, NY: New City, 1991), 385.

7. An exception to this trend was Cistercian bridal mysticism, growing out of the invention of romantic love in the Middle Ages. At the Reformation, faith replaced love, and humility prevailed along with it.

8. Gregory of Nyssa, "On the Holy Trinity, and of the Godhead of the Holy Spirit," in *Nicene and Post-Nicene Fathers*, Series 2, ed. P. Schaff and H. Wace, 14 vols. (1890–1900; repr., Peabody, MA: Hendrickson, 1994), 5:326–30.

9. Ibid., 5:329.

10. In light of this, Zizioulas's attribution of the anti-Platonic ontological revolution of the Greek Fathers may call for nuancing.

11. Augustine, *Confessions*, trans. Vernon J. Bourke (New York: Fathers of the Church, Inc., 1953), 4.

12. Basil of Caesarea, *On the Holy Spirit* (New York: St. Vladimir's Seminary Press, 1980), 44.

13. Pseudo-Dionysius, *The Complete Works*, ed. P. Rorem, Classics of Western Spirituality (New York: Paulist Press, 1987), 75.

14. Ibid., 54.

15. Ibid., 74.

16. Ibid., 77.

Chapter 9: Deep Wisdom

1. Barbara Brown Taylor, *Home by Another Way* (Cambridge, MA: Cowley Publications, 1999), 38.

2. Jürgen Moltmann, *The Crucified God* (San Francisco: Harper & Row, 1974), 40.

Contributors

Gerald L. Bray (B.A., McGill University; M.Litt., D.Litt., University of Paris-Sorbonne) is Anglican Professor of Divinity at Beeson Divinity School of Samford University, where he teaches church history, historical theology, and Latin. He has published many scholarly articles and books, including *The Doctrine of God* in the Contours of Christian Theology series (of which he is general editor); *Creeds, Councils, and Christ*; and *Biblical Interpretation: Past and Present*; as well as three volumes in the Ancient Christian Commentary Series. Most recently he has edited the *Records of Convocation, the Acts of the Synods of the Churches of England and Ireland from the Middle Ages to the Nineteenth Century.*

Ellen T. Charry (B.A., Barnard College; Ph.D., Temple University) is the Margaret W. Harmon Associate Professor of Systematic and Historical Theology at Princeton Theological Seminary. She is immediate past editor of *Theology Today* and serves as editor-at-large for *Christian Century.* Her most recent books are *Inquiring after God: Classic and Contemporary Readings* and *By the Renewing of Your Minds: The Pastoral Function of Christian Doctrine.*

Avery Cardinal Dulles, S.J. (A.B., Harvard University; Ph.L., S.T.L., Woodstock; S.T.D., Gregorian), is the Lawrence J. McGinley Professor in Religion and Society at Fordham University. The author of over 750 articles on theological topics, Cardinal Dulles has published many books, including *A Testimonial to Grace*;

167

Models of the Church; *A History of Apologetics*; *The Assurance of Things Hoped For*; and *The Splendor of Faith: The Theological Vision of Pope John Paul II*.

Timothy George (A.B., University of Tennessee; M.Div., Harvard Divinity School; Th.D., Harvard University) is the founding dean of Beeson Divinity School of Samford University. He serves as executive editor for *Christianity Today* and on numerous advisory boards. A prolific author, he contributes regularly to scholarly journals. His many books include *Galatians*; *Theology of the Reformers*; and *Is the Father of Jesus the God of Muhummad?*

James Earl Massey (B.R.E., Detroit Bible College; M.A., Oberlin Graduate School of Theology; Hum.D., Tuskegee University; Litt.D., Anderson University) is dean emeritus and distinguished professor-at-large of the Anderson University School of Theology. He has served on editorial boards of *Preaching* and *Leadership* and *Christianity Today*. He has published many books, including *Designing the Sermon: Order and Movement in Preaching*; *Sundays in Tuskegee Chapel: Selected Sermons*; *The Burdensome Joy of Preaching*; and most recently his autobiography, *Aspects of My Pilgrimage*.

Frederica Mathewes-Green (B.A., University of South Carolina; M.A., Virginia Episcopal Seminary) is perhaps known best as a commentator on National Public Radio's *Morning Edition*. She is a regular contributor to *Christianity Today*; *National Review Online*; *First Things*; and *Touchstone*. She has written many books, some of her most beloved ones including *The Open Door: Entering the Sanctuary of Icons and Prayer*; *The Illuminated Heart: The Ancient Christian Path of Transformation*; and *Facing East: A Pilgrim's Journey into the Mysteries of Orthodoxy*.

Alister E. McGrath (B.A., B.D., M.A., D.D., D.Phil., Oxford University) is professor of historical theology at Oxford University and president of the Oxford Center for Evangelism and Apologetics. He is an expert both on the history of Christian thought, especially in the sixteenth and early seventeenth century, and on systematic theology in general, and has been featured regularly in radio and television programs in England and abroad. He is the author of many books, including *Bridge-Building: Effective Christian Apologetics* and *Christian Theology: An Introduction*. His most recent work of systematic theology is a three-volume series, with volumes entitled *Nature*, *Reality*, and *Theory*.

J. I. Packer (B.A., M.A., D.Phil., Oxford University) is the Board of Governors' Professor, Theology, at Regent College, Vancouver. He serves as a senior editor and visiting scholar of *Christianity Today* and contributes to a variety of theological journals. The author of many books, his most beloved works include *Faithfulness and Holiness: The Witness of J. C. Ryle*; *God's Plans for You*; *Knowing Christianity*; *Knowing God*; and *Knowing and Doing God's Will: Daily Devotions for Every Day of the Year.*

Cornelius Plantinga Jr. (A.B., Calvin College; B.D., Calvin Theological Seminary; Ph.D., Princeton Theological Seminary) is president and Charles W. Colson Professor of Theology at Calvin Theological Seminary. He is former editor of the *Calvin Theological Journal* and current member of the board of editors of *Books & Culture*. In addition to publishing numerous articles, his books include *Not the Way It's Supposed to Be: A Breviary of Sin*; *Beyond Doubt: Faith-Building Devotion on Questions Christians Ask*; and *Engaging God's World: A Christian View of Faith.*

Index